IMAGINE

FINANCIAL SECURITY
FOR LIFE

BRENT WELCH

IMAGINE

FINANCIAL SECURITY
FOR LIFE

Helping You Retire with Confidence and Peace

Published by Advantage, Charleston, South Carolina.
Member of Advantage Media Group.

ADVANTAGE is a registered trademark and the Advantage colophon is a trademark of Advantage Media Group, Inc.

Printed in the United States of America.

ISBN: 978-1-59932-577-4
LCCN: 2015945758

Book design by Megan Elger.

This publication is designed to provide accurate and authoritative information in regard to the subject matter covered. It is sold with the understanding that the publisher is not engaged in rendering legal, accounting, or other professional services. If legal advice or other expert assistance is required, the services of a competent professional person should be sought.

At the time of this publication the Author, Brent J. Welch, is an Investment Advisor Representative of Welshire Capital, Inc., a Registered Investment Advisor located in WI, 1113 Riders Club Road, Onalaska, WI 54650, 608-783-0003 and 999 Fourier Drive, Suite 100, Madison, WI 53713, 608-841-1043. Mr. Welch is also a Registered Representative of, and offers securities through, Comprehensive Asset Management and Servicing, Inc., ("CAMAS") Member FINRA/SIPC, 2001 Route 46, Suite 506, Parsippany, NJ 07054, 973-394-0404. The opinions and views expressed herein are those exclusively of the Author and not of Welshire Capital, LLC or CAMAS. This book is written for informational purposes only and is not meant to provide specific investment, tax or legal advice. Nothing in this publication should be construed as an offer to buy or sell securities. Investments in securities carry risks, including the loss of principal.

Advantage Media Group is proud to be a part of the Tree Neutral® program. Tree Neutral offsets the number of trees consumed in the production and printing of this book by taking proactive steps such as planting trees in direct proportion to the number of trees used to print books. To learn more about Tree Neutral, please visit **www.treeneutral.com**. To learn more about Advantage's commitment to being a responsible steward of the environment, please visit **www.advantagefamily.com/green**

Advantage Media Group is a publisher of business, self-improvement, and professional development books and online learning. We help entrepreneurs, business leaders, and professionals share their Stories, Passion, and Knowledge to help others Learn & Grow. Do you have a manuscript or book idea that you would like us to consider for publishing? Please visit **advantagefamily.com** or call **1.866.775.1696.**

To you, my extraordinary clients. You are kind, nice, smart, faithful, particular, and enjoy personable service the way you deserve it. You have taught me about faith, family, friends, having fun, and being philanthropic. Thank you! I deeply appreciate you, admire you, and extend love to you.

ACKNOWLEDGMENTS

First of all, I acknowledge God, because He gave me the framework for this book from the Bible as written in Ecclesiastes 11:2. Through God's leadership, I met Greg Taylor, who put me in touch with Advantage, my publisher.

Thanks to Regina Roths and the whole Advantage team for your help in making this project happen. I also thank my wife, family, friends, and clients for your help and encouragement. Marianne, you have loved, supported, and helped me to be who I am today. Since 1986, you have helped me understand and communicate clearly what I am thinking and feeling. I love you babe. My mom and dad, Jann and Jack Welch; you are both definitely front and center in my acknowledgments. I admire your faith and family values. Your love and service for others, your entrepreneurial spirit, sincere faith, and never-give-up work ethic has sprouted wings and flies within me. Thanks to my whole Welshire[SM] team; I appreciate, love, and respect you all. I soar with everyone in my life who helps me be who I am today.

TABLE OF CONTENTS

FOREWORD

by Jake Welch

I have enjoyed sports my whole life. After playing for many different coaches and in many different leagues, I've come to realize that sports have a lot in common with retirement planning.

One of my earliest memories was learning the secret to competing and winning at a father-son basketball camp in Madison. My coaches included Bo Ryan, Dick Bennett, and Tony Bennett. They always built brilliant defensive game plans that brought out the best in their players—they were especially attuned to strategic positioning of each member of the defensive team.

Similarly, retirement planning can help you incorporate defensive strategies into your investments so that you may position yourself against the roadblock of stock market volatility.

Later, in high school, I competed for a state championship-caliber football program in which I learned that a team is composed of many moving parts, and success is achieved when everyone works together. This starts with an offensive line providing flawless blocking to protect the team's greatest asset, its quarterback. This is particularly important for a quarterback nearing retirement, who is undoubtedly experiencing less agility than he did in his youth.

A good offense is also key when retirement is in sight and financial mobility is in decline; this may be the time to consider refocusing your risk tolerance from capital growth to capital preservation to help ensure that your investments stay in good standing.

Finally, while playing wide receiver for the University of Wisconsin–La Crosse, I learned the true meaning of teamwork. In order to win, you have to present a unified front. To help ensure that you are prepared for success and adversity in retirement, it is advisable to have expertise overseeing each aspect of your retirement planning. This could include a financial team composed of your accountant, CPA, attorney, banker, insurance agent, and retirement advisor.

College sports also taught me that championship teams can always be attributed to strong leadership and coaching. Likewise, an advisor will help you prepare to succeed in retirement by ensuring you have an exceptional team working with you toward your goals. Your advisor should help you match your assets with your trusts or estate and will help you take care of your money so that you can focus your time and energy on things that are more important to you, such as your faith, family, and friends.

Imagine Financial Security for Life outlines Eight Investment Strategies for Life and provides details that may help you overcome some of the roadblocks that lie ahead. My father, Brent Welch, draws from over three decades of experience in creating retirement game plans. I hope you enjoy this book; Brent will discuss how you may be better prepared for the roadblocks that may keep you from financial security and peace. You are in charge of your retirement, and you deserve a team that can help you make smarter choices with your money.

INTRODUCTION

Emotions really help define the fact that we're human—that we're alive. We face extreme emotions of joy and exuberance when we're riding a roller coaster, getting married, attending a child's graduation, or holding a newborn baby and marveling at a beautiful new life in this world. At times, our emotions include sadness and grief, such as when we feel we've failed at achieving a goal or when we lose a loved one.

Different emotions really help us know that we're experiencing life to its fullest. Wouldn't you prefer to live your life with more confidence and peace?

In the world of investing, emotions may not be your friend. Emotions often cause investors to make horrible decisions, such as selling when the market is low and buying when the market is high. You may be inclined to do exactly the opposite of what you should do because of emotions.

According to Dalbar's Quantitative Analysis of Investor Behavior (QAIB), for the past three decades the average American stock fund investor has underperformed by more than 7 percent; during a period when the S&P 500 was returning 11 percent per annum, investors were earning only 3.7 percent.

My goal is to help educate you to make smarter choices with your money so that you can move toward living life with more confidence and peace. I want to help you create plans and strategies that may help you eliminate worry and live your life to the fullest.

A WORLD OF UNCERTAINTY

People are concerned about their futures and with good reason.

The United States has over $18 trillion of debt, according to JP Morgan Investments and *The Economist* magazine; we're adding $1.469 trillion of fresh debt every year due to quantitative easing ($900 billion) and deficit spending ($469 billion). At this rate, by the time our nation's administration changes hands, we'll be over $20 trillion in debt! I encourage you to look for yourself at www.usdebtclock.org.

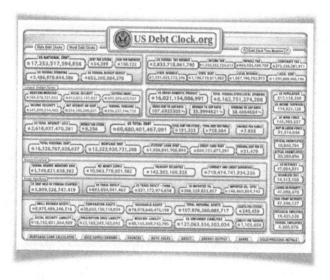

My concern is that if interest rates once again approach 10 percent, we'll be looking at $2 trillion in interest payments on the debt, which is over half of America's $3.8 billion annual budget. The country will not have enough money to go around, and something will have to give. What will we be unable to pay? Medicare or Medicaid? Defense, Social Security, or national health care?

Another concern, shared by many people, is that while inflation and average tax rates have been low recently, both have historically been much higher.

Then there's the issue of longevity; simply put, people are living longer. Advances in technology are keeping us alive longer, but that blessing becomes an additional challenge to our security.

WE KNOW WHERE YOU'RE COMING FROM

At Welshire Capital^{SM}, we know you're worried about these things; we're concerned about them, too.

As the founder and managing partner of Welshire Capital^{SM}, a firm focusing on private wealth management, retirement, and estate planning, I empathize with the financial concerns people have. I and the other members of the Welshire Capital^{SM} team love to help people feel more secure about their financial futures.

Welshire Capital^{SM} serves over 500 families in more than a dozen states. We're deeply concerned about the financial futures of our clients, and we want to take care of them the way we want to be taken care of.

Instead of asking clients to buy, hold, and hope, we at Welshire Capital^{SM} aim to take action in anticipation of the stock market falling apart or the economy going up in flames. When you face tough times ahead, we believe your advisor should have prepared you instead of doing nothing.

This book grew out of more than three decades of experience as a retirement planner. I thank God for that experience and my education as a Certified Financial Planner® practitioner, Chartered Retirement Planning Specialist®, Chartered Financial Consultant, Chartered Life Underwriter, and Accredited Investment Fiduciary®.

Most people retire once, but I've had the distinct privilege of retiring hundreds of times over 30 years with my clients. I've seen them before retirement, through retirement, and helped their families when a loved one dies. I've assisted widowed clients and also their devastated children when they ultimately pass away.

From these experiences—all these meetings with clients and helping them plan their futures—I found myself wanting to come up with something to combat "stock market terrorism," the chaos that the stock market may create in their emotional life. Part of the battle is about doing something smarter with our clients' retirement money.

So back in 2007, we at Welshire Capital^{SM} began what we call the "Advance and Protect Strategy," which involves helping our clients work toward keeping their money in the right place at the right time. That strategy turned out to be the first of many investment "seat belts" or "air bags" we use to help protect our clients' interests. We formulated the Eight Investment Strategies for Life to help inform clients to make smarter choices with their money. Our passion is to help our clients experience more financial security and peace in their lives.

USING STRATEGY TO OVERCOME EMOTION

We work best with folks who are centered on what we call "The Five Fs": faith, family, friends, having fun, and being philanthropic. Folks who are nice, generous, and focused on helping others tend to be more philanthropic. As mutual fund pioneer and philanthropist John Templeton used to say, "It's nice to be important, but it's more important to be nice."

Our clients tend to be people who've worked their entire lives and built up a retirement nest egg; many have paid off their homes and made a lot of good decisions in their life. They've accumulated wealth by being a bit more aggressive in a capital growth mode. Most of our clients don't consider themselves ultra-wealthy although they may have millions.

But when they retire, their investment objectives often change from capital growth to capital preservation: they want to keep together what they've worked so hard to put together.

When we custom design a portfolio for you, we base it on your risk tolerance, from conservative to aggressive. We subscribe to the school of belief that your asset allocation is the most important aspect of determining your success, and we work with three types of investment strategies—high-risk, moderate-risk, and safe strategies—to create a portfolio that is protected against disaster.

In short, we may help you increase your guaranteed income to take care of your fixed standard-of-living expenses. Then, we work to make sure you also have funds available for the fun things in life, such as travel or discretionary expenses like gifts and entertainment. Finally, we want to work with your CPA and attorney to make sure your estate and asset protection plans coordinate with your wealth management plans.

Studies have shown that investing in the market is commonly driven by emotion. We handle the emotions of investing by helping you create a portfolio that is designed to do well in any market environment. We use strategies for anticipating challenges in the market and protecting your money during those times. For example, if the market is going down, we want to make sure that some of your investments have principal that's protected against downside risk and that you have guaranteed income for life.

I'll go into more detail about the strategies we use in the chapters that follow, but among them is something we call "investment air bags." Like the air bags in your car that deploy to save you in the event of an accident, these income guarantees wrap a separate account, such as a mutual fund, to ensure you have income even if the primary account drops. We also can add a "seat belt" to your investments called AssetLock, a technology that uses formulas rather than guesswork to reduce the downside risk of investing and helps take the emotions out of the equation.

TRUST AND VERIFY

When I was in middle school, my teachers asked me what I wanted to do when I grew up, and I always told them I wanted to do something that helped people. This business gives me the opportunity to help others in a more personal and confidential manner. We get to know our clients up close and personal, and because of that mutual trust, we're able to understand the intricacies of our clients' financial affairs

That's a real privilege. It gives us a platform to help people be in control of their retirement and get answers to questions such as:

- Will my money run out?
- Do I have enough?
- Am I on track?

You deserve to know the answers to these key questions.

It has been said that there's a cost for creating a plan and a cost for not planning, and quite often the cost for not planning is much higher. Or maybe you've heard it put another way: nobody plans to fail, they just fail to plan. Creating a plan can help you get on track and stay on track with your retirement planning.

While it's important to trust your financial advisor, you also need to verify the information. That's a lesson I learned from a client who was able to retire from a major telecommunications company at 55 with $1.5 million for her retirement. Her boss always told her to trust the vendors she worked with but also to verify information so that she knew it was correct. Sue and I developed a really good relationship based on trust, because she's been able to verify what I've told her every step of the way.

That lesson also complements one I learned from my dad. When I started in this business back in 1984 he wouldn't just take my recommendations.

He instead made me go back, sharpen my pencil, and come up with three different options that he could choose from. He taught me a practice we use at Welshire^{SM} that we call "We guide and help you decide." Because of my dad, we give you a menu of choices, along with our advice, and then we let you be in control of what you do. You can choose to implement some of the strategies, none of them, or all of them, and then you can implement them yourself, with someone else's help, or with our assistance.

ROADBLOCKS AND STRATEGIES

This book contains information to help you overcome fears about financial insecurity and discusses how you can increase your confidence and sense of peace during these precarious economic times. Eight of the chapters address the roadblocks that can keep you from feeling secure, followed by another eight chapters discussing strategies that may help you protect your wealth from ruin.

This is the information we use in our workshops, which we've been conducting in Wisconsin for more than 25 years. In these classes, we discuss tax, investment, retirement and estate planning. Our goal is to help you retire with more confidence and peace.

For most of the workshops, we invite folks between the ages of 54 and 70. We discuss roadblocks, strategies, and other factors impacting your retirement. What we're really offering is a sense of comfort about your retirement. By giving you answers to your questions along with solutions designed to help you retire with a secure financial plan, you'll be better equipped to remove the emotion from your decision making. You deserve to have a plan that will help you retire with financial security and peace.

TIME TRAVEL INVESTING— WORDS FROM THE WISE

Imagine if you had a time travel application on your smartphone that would allow you to go back in time and talk to some very wise people about finances. Who are some of the people you would like to visit, and what do you think they would say to you?

I envisioned time travel investing myself in order to meet with King Solomon, who in Ecclesiastes 11:2 said, "Invest in seven ventures, yes, in eight; you do not know what disaster may come upon the land." That advice is 3,000 years old, yet it's still applicable today.

If you were to sit with King Solomon, what would he tell you that would be an investment strategy that may work today?

I think he would first ask some questions, such as: "What do you want to accomplish with your money?" or "What are some concerns that you have?"

To which your answer might be: "Taxes are getting higher, inflation is around the corner, the stock market has once again hit new highs and may plummet again, and people are living longer. One of my greatest fears is that I'm going to outlive my money. Solomon, what can I do about this?"

I believe he would advise looking at strategies that are available and then break them into three categories: growth, moderate risk, and safe strategies.

Growth strategies, he may have explained, include dividend-paying stocks designed to generate an income flow for you as an investor, even when stocks are flat or down. This income stream may help you pay your bills during extended bleak periods of the stock market, and it may help you overcome inflation and concerns about outliving your money. Moderate strategies may help you protect your money from stock market volatility, political unrest, and global economic challenges. And safe strategies might alleviate your concerns about the high cost of long-term care, old-age illness, and longevity. Together, these strategies may help you overcome some of the concerns that may keep you awake at night.

THE REALITY OF RISK

There are a lot of risks that you face in your investing, including systemic and nonsystemic risk. Systemic risks include systems that affect your money, such as the stock market, taxes, inflation, and interest rates. Nonsystemic risks include business risks, for example, having all your investments in one company that ultimately may be poorly managed and teeter into bankruptcy. Other nonsystemic risks that could impact your financial future include old age or the high cost of long-term care. You may die too soon, live too long, or get disabled along the way. If you developed a terminal illness, such as Alzheimer's, it could eat up your assets and destroy your finances.

Even if you hid all your money in your house or buried it in the backyard, there's still risk: it could decompose, be stolen, or burn up in a fire. Again, these aren't systems, but they're still risks that you face no matter what you do with your money.

Every investment you make comes with risk. The question is always this: Is the risk greater or less than other investments, and is the reward greater or less? So with each investment you make, you should consider the "opportunity cost," which is the difference in return between the types of investments you choose. What that means is, if you put money into one investment, you can't put it in another, so how much return or how much safety are you potentially passing up? This is a factor that must be weighed anytime you invest.

WHAT WORKED?

While we're traveling back in time, let's look at some of the investments that performed well even during the most difficult economic times, for example, the Great Depression, the flat decade of the 1970s, or in 1986, when there was a huge one-day drop in the market.

Common sense would tell us that even in the toughest of times people still buy products they need such as soap, food, and electricity. That may be why these stocks always seem to make money. It's like during the gold rush—not everybody struck gold, but the hardware stores made money selling shovels and other tools regardless. Certain segments of our economy tend to do well even when other segments don't.

Now, using the time travel app on your smartphone, go back in time and explore the advice of other people who have influenced you. Who in your past has made an impact on the way you view and manage your finances? What lessons did you learn from them? What one word would you use to describe the way they managed their money? I've been fortunate to rub shoulders with businessmen who are billionaires, and my conversations with them have been quite impactful. Still traveling back in time, look at your financial history and some of the investments and decisions you've made. What could you have done differently back then that would have made things better financially today?

Even some of the nation's wealthiest people had to learn from mistakes. Take for example the Rockefeller family. John D. Rockefeller Sr., the industrialist, had an estate valued at $26,410,837. The estate taxes and costs of probating his estate were approximately 70 percent or $18,487,586, according to the *New York Times*, PBS, *TIME*, and InsuranceNetNews. However, J.D. Rockefeller Jr. learned from his father's mistakes. He learned how to use advanced strategies to protect his assets, so he lost only 16 percent of his estate to taxes; his estate of $160,598,584 was taxed $24,965,954.

There are a lot of people over time who taught us great lessons about money. For example, Ben Franklin's wisdom about money is undisputed, and sitting at his feet you would learn that even a small hole—unaccounted-for expenses—could sink a great financial ship.

On the other side of the coin, use the time travel app on your smartphone to remember some of the best things you ever did financially. What were those investments? What did you do right? Can you build on your successes? If you can picture in your mind what those decisions did for your financial security, what one word would you use to describe the feeling you get when you think of that image?

Now use the app to project yourself into the future. Where would you like to be three years from now personally, professionally, and financially? What would have to happen in your personal, professional, and financial life for you to be on track? What are you doing today to ensure you're where you want and need to be three, five, or ten years from now?

If the costs of hiring a retirement wealth advisor are a concern for you, let me reiterate the words of Ben Feldman: "It costs something to do something and it costs something to do nothing. Quite often, doing nothing costs much more."

THE EIGHT ROADBLOCKS AND EIGHT STRATEGIES

When I read King Solomon's statement about investing in eight strategies, it jumped out at me, and I immediately pulled out an index card and drew seven lines down the card creating eight columns. At the top of the index card I wrote: Eight Investment Strategies for Life.

The chapters that follow discuss the roadblocks that keep people from feeling safe and the strategies for combating your financial fears and insecurities.

The eight roadblocks are easily remembered by the abbreviation STOP RUIN, which stands for stocks, taxes, old-age illness, procrastination, running out of money, unstable economy, inflation, and no plan. The eight strategies include three high-risk strategies (individual stocks, exchange-traded funds, and mutual funds), two moderate-risk strategies (investment air bags and AssetLock), and three safe strategies (fixed index annuities, guaranteed income riders, and asset-based long-term care insurance).

What's important when it comes to investing is to put your money in a variety of different strategies. You can still use the same common sense principles to guide your decision process, but you have new strategies available to you that you may not have had available to you before.

Now let's look at the eight roadblocks to financial security and peace.

CHAPTER 1 TAKEAWAYS:

WHAT ARE THE TOP THREE THINGS YOU WOULD CHANGE IN YOUR INVESTING HISTORY?

_____

_____

_____

_____

_____

_____

_____

_____

_____

NAME SOME PEOPLE WHO HAVE INFLUENCED YOU TO MAKE THE PROPER FINANCIAL DECISIONS. WHAT WAS THEIR ADVICE? WHAT HAS BEEN THE RESULT?

_____

_____

_____

_____

_____

_____

_____

_____

_____

WHAT NEEDS TO HAPPEN OVER THE NEXT THREE YEARS IN YOUR PERSONAL, PROFESSIONAL, AND FINANCIAL LIVES FOR YOU TO BE ON TRACK?

Personal:_____

_____

_____

_____

Professional:_____

_____

_____

_____

Financial:_____

_____

_____

_____

ROADBLOCK	STRATEGY
Stock market losses	AssetLock or Welshire^{SM} Advance & Protect Investment air bags Asset-based long-term care insurance Fixed index annuities Guaranteed income riders
Taxes	Stocks ETFs Mutual funds Investment air bags Asset-based long-term care insurance Fixed index annuities
Old-age illness	Stocks ETFs Mutual funds AssetLock or Welshire^{SM} Advance & Protect Investment air bags Asset-based long-term care insurance Fixed index annuities Guaranteed income riders
Procrastination	Overcoming procrastination means just getting started with any of the investment strategies for life Stocks ETFs Mutual funds AssetLock or Welshire^{SM} Advance & Protect Investment air bags Asset-based long-term care insurance Fixed index annuities Guaranteed income riders.

Running out of money	Stocks ETFs Mutual funds AssetLock or Welshire[SM] Advance & Protect Investment air bags Asset-based long-term care insurance Fixed index annuities Guaranteed income riders
Unstable economy	Stocks ETFs Mutual funds AssetLock or Welshire[SM] Advance & Protect Investment air bags Asset-based long-term care insurance Fixed index annuities Guaranteed income riders
Inflation	Stocks ETFs Mutual funds AssetLock or Welshire[SM] Advance & Protect Investment air bags Asset-based long-term care insurance Fixed index annuities Guaranteed income riders
No plan	No one plans to fail; they fail to plan using any of the Eight Investment Strategies for Life

ROADBLOCK #1—STOCK MARKET LOSSES

ADVENTURES IN INVESTING

We'll ultimately discuss strategies to help you increase confidence during these precarious times, but first, let's look at what I've identified as eight roadblocks to financial security and peace. Each of the next eight chapters discusses one of these roadblocks.

The first roadblock is stock market losses.

MARKET VOLATILITY

Investors today understand volatility more than the investors did during the greatest bull market of all time, from 1984 to 2000. Consider the wild ride occurring in the market since 1997: it has been up 106 percent, down 49 percent, up 101 percent, down 57 percent, and then up well over 200 percent through the first half of 2015. When the market goes up, down, up, down, and up again, what do you think it will do next?

When investing in the stock market, the most important thing you need to understand is your own pain points: Are you in more pain when you're fully invested in the stock market and it drops 50 percent? Or are you in more pain when you're not fully invested in the market and it goes up 50 percent? In other words, would you rather avoid stock market losses, or would you rather make sure you're fully onboard with all gains?

If you're an aggressive investor, does it hurt more to be out of the market? When the market drops and everyone else is upset, you're in there buying all those stocks at low prices. If you're a low-risk investor, you get nervous when the stock market drops. You're the type of investor who is happier with more investments that guarantee an income—with the return of your money being more important than the return on your money.

It is important to remember that you can't have it both ways; you cannot fully participate in stock market gains without accepting the downside risk of the market.

BULLS AND BEARS

Simply put, a bull market goes up, a bear market goes down. A bull or bear market that goes on for an extended period of time is called a secular bull or bear market. Within a secular market, there might be cyclical markets; for example, within a secular bear there might be cyclical bulls.

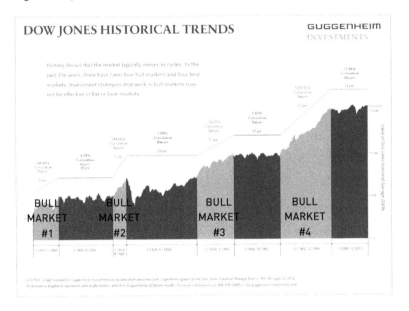

According to Guggenheim Investments, since 1897 the stock market (as measured by the Dow Jones Industrial Average) has had only four bull markets. The first, from 1897 to 1906, grew by 149 percent; the second, from 1924 to 1929 (the roaring '20s), increased 295 percent; and the third, during the nifty fifties from 1954 to 1966, gained 154 percent. The best bull market of all times exploded to the upside by 1,059 percent and lasted a full 17 years, from 1982 until 2000.

Since the peak of 2007, the market has been up 45 percent. Since the lull of 2009, it was up 224 percent.

Should you invest when the market is going down? Well, that's a little like catching a falling knife—it might be safer to wait until it hits the ground. A stock that's in a bear market might not be a logical choice; it might behave erratically. You can't trust that a bear market will rebound just because the underlying economy is strong. Too often, it has done just the opposite.

In short, the stock market is an emotional roller coaster. When the market is down, there's fear, when it begins to go up, there's enthusiasm, and when it peaks, there's irrational exuberance. People buy when stocks are priced high, and they usually sell out of fear.

Warren Buffet figured this out, and that's one of the main reasons why he's done so well. He has said that investors should "be fearful when others are greedy and greedy when others are fearful." Basically the antithesis of what the average individual investor does. So back in 2008 and 2009, Buffet was buying up stocks in companies when everybody else was running away from them.

This is an example of the emotional side of investing. It's such a weighty subject that theories in behavioral economics have netted a Nobel Prize in recent years.

Other theories about the stock market include a prominent one by John Bogle, chairman and founder of Vanguard Funds, who says we may witness two drops of up to 50 percent in the stock market over the next ten years, as reported by "CNBC Halftime Report" on April 1, 2013. Another brilliant investment manager,

Bill Gross, founder and chairman of PIMCO Funds, said in a July 31, 2012, article on Fortune.com that, "Stocks were a Ponzi scheme for the last 100 years."

BE PREPARED

The bottom line is that you need to be prepared for whatever the market throws at you, because the stock market will go up and will go down.

Our economy is fueled by borrowed money; essentially, the gas that's in the tank of the economy is borrowed, and because of that, we might run out down the road. That's going to cause the economic engine to stop at some point—or else be refueled by more borrowed money or more printed money, which puts us in an even more precarious position. The more money we borrow, the higher inflation may rise and interest rates climb. The more money we print, the more volatility we experience in currency fluctuations and oftentimes in the stock market.

So in the future we need to be ready for wild swings in the market, and we're looking at living through those during our retirement. That's why we recommend the Eight Investment Strategies for Life—to help reduce the emotional wreckage that's caused by an unpredictable, erratic stock market, which can skyrocket one day and plummet the next.

The reality is, investing in the stock market may feel like a psychotic venture. Sometimes even when all the fundamentals are solid and it looks like it should be recovering, the stock market just keeps crashing. Or it continues to go up when all the leading indicators are saying it should be going down. It has a life of its own, and you can't predict it; you just have to bear with what it gives you. But if you rely on the stock market alone for your sustenance and your postretirement years, you're likely going to be very emotionally distraught. And who wants to be unable to sleep at night when you're retired?

CHAPTER 2 TAKEAWAYS:

DESCRIBE THE EMOTIONS YOU HAVE IN
RELATION TO THE FOLLOWING:

The stock market plunges. _____

_____

_____

_____

The stock market hits record highs. _____

_____

_____

_____

Terrorists attacked the World Trade Center. _____

_____

_____

_____

Congress borrowing trillions of dollars each year to operate. ___

_____

_____

_____

The fiscal cliff or other money problems caused by an unbalanced
budget. _____

_____

_____

You experience illness. _____

_____

_____

_____

A close loved one dies. _____

_____

_____

_____

You spend time and have fun with family and friends. _____

_____

_____

_____

You give to a charitable cause that really needs it. _____

_____

_____

_____

HOW DO ALL THOSE EMOTIONS RELATE TO YOUR MONEY?

_____

_____

_____

CAN YOU AFFORD TO GO THROUGH ANOTHER
50 PERCENT DROP IN THE STOCK MARKET?

_____

_____

_____

WHAT WOULD IT FEEL LIKE TO TAKE THE EMOTIONS
OUT OF INVESTING AND TO HAVE A PLATFORM
WHERE YOU MIGHT EXPERIENCE SUCCESS?

_____

_____

_____

WHAT KIND OF INVESTMENT "AIR BAGS" AND "SEAT BELTS" DO YOU HAVE FOR YOUR MONEY?

_____

_____

_____

HOW MUCH GUARANTEED INCOME DO YOU PREDICT YOU'LL NEED EACH YEAR DURING RETIREMENT?

_____

_____

_____

CHAPTER 3

ROADBLOCK #2—TAXES

WILL YOUR FUTURE BE PUMMELED?

Taxes are the second roadblock that should be minimized in order to strive for financial security.

Let's start by considering this: Do you think taxes are going up or down? When I give my workshops, I ask this question, and the answer is generally unanimous—everyone thinks taxes are going up.

Why is this? It's all the reasons we mentioned earlier: the deficit, printing too much money, inflation, Congress lowering taxes to stimulate the economy—all of these factors may cause taxes to go up in the future. It's the cost of running our government. We're not revenue neutral; we're still running a deficit economy, which calls for higher taxes.

With deficits ballooning, Congress is addicted to the pursuit of more revenue. The Tax Foundation archives historical marginal tax rates dating back to 1913. The top marginal federal tax rate from 1913 to 1915 was just 7 percent. From 1916 to 1917, the top federal tax rate skyrocketed from 15 percent to 67 percent. Then, from 1918 to 1922, it hovered around 60 percent before dropping back under 20 percent by 1927. For 2015, the highest marginal rate was posted at 39.6 percent.

HIGHEST MARGINAL TAX RATES 1913–2015

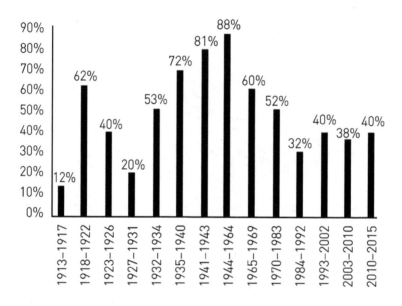

Source: IRS.gov (table compiled by author)

The fact is, since 1913, the top marginal rate averaged about 50 percent.

With the chance that taxes will go up in the future, what does that mean for you and your money?

Three scenarios follow that demonstrate how you might avoid higher taxes in the future. In addition to these scenarios, there are also estate tax strategies that may allow you to avoid estate taxes for dying in America—if your estate is more than $10.86 million as a married couple, you may pay to up to 40 percent of your estate in death taxes. Not only can you play the shell game with taxes, but you can also play the game with capital gains taxes after you die. As the Honorable Learned Hand, former US appeals court justice said, "There are two systems of taxation in our country: one for the informed and one for the uninformed."

SCENARIO #1—MAXING OUT TAX DEDUCTIBLE INVESTMENTS

In 2015, a farmer sold the mineral rights to his property for $400,000, which netted him approximately $300,000 after capital gains taxes.

To invest his net gain, I suggested as his financial advisor that he max out his current 401(k) plan so that he could get a tax deduction on the capital gains in the current year. Then, for the following year, he should max out his Roth 401(k) plan, because that year he could put $24,000 into the account. That same year, he and his spouse could put $13,000 into their Roth IRAs. This solution would allow some of the money to be tax deferred, some of it to be in growth strategies, and some of it to fund the farmer's future by maxing out his 401(k) plan.

At the time, he was only putting about $12,000 into his Roth 401(k), so when I suggested that he double his retirement savings, he nervously replied that he couldn't afford to do so.

I told him, "Well, yes, you can. You can live off $1,000 a month from the money you got for mineral rights in your savings account and contribute an additional $1,000 per month from your paycheck to your 401(k). You take the 401(k) contribution out of your paycheck because the only way you can get funds into a 401(k) is through payroll deduction. Then you're actually living off your savings account for that extra $1,000 a month." But again, it's about moving it, essentially, from the right pocket to the left. It's moving it from a savings account into a 401(k) plan but doing it through your paycheck and then living on your cash.

Then I suggested that he shift is 2016 charitable contributions to 2015 and double up his other deductible expenses. He should max out his traditional 401(k) plan and IRAs in the year he receives the check for selling his mineral rights. He may feel more comfortable living off his savings for the next couple of years if he keeps in mind that he is maxing out all of his tax-advantaged retirement plans.

SCENARIO #2—KEEPING CAPITAL GAINS TAXES LOW UPON DEATH

Twenty years ago, a couple invested $30,000 into a stock called Fastenal. From time to time Fastenal has reportedly grown faster than Apple stock, turning their $30,000 investment into more than $2 million.

If one spouse sold their stock today, the capital gains tax would be nearly $600,000. If they both hold it until the first spouse dies, there may be zero taxes, because the state in which they live is a marital property state. If the couple holds the Fastenal stock in the form of "survivorship marital property" through a special marital property agreement, then they may receive a full step-up basis on the stock at the first spouse's death.

That little strategy just might save their family $600,000 in capital gains taxes. Since the couple has done such a great job saving money during their working years, they don't really need the Fastenal stock to live on. So they may be able to hold the stock until the first spouse dies as a capital gains tax-avoidance strategy.

SCENARIO #3—SAVING ON REAL ESTATE TAXES

You can also reduce your real estate taxes by moving to a state with lower real estate taxes. According to the taxes.about.com website, there are ten states with low real estate taxes. The top ten best states for property taxes along with the percentage of home value paid in property taxes is:

1. Louisiana - 0.18%
2. Hawaii - 0.26%
3. Alabama - 0.33%
4. Delaware - 0.43%
5. West Virginia - 0.49%
6. South Carolina - 0.50%
7. Arkansas - 0.52%
8. Mississippi - 0.52%
9. New Mexico - 0.55%
10. Wyoming - 0.58%

The Tax Foundation found that homeowners in these states paid the most in property taxes compared to home value. The percentages represent the percentage of home value that homeowners pay in property taxes.

1. New Jersey - 1.89%
2. New Hampshire - 1.86%
3. Texas - 1.81%
4. Wisconsin - 1.76%
5. Nebraska - 1.70%
6. Illinois - 1.73%
7. Connecticut - 1.63%
8. Michigan - 1.62%
9. Vermont - 1.59%
10. North Dakota - 1.42%

In other words, if you live in a $300,000 home in Wisconsin you will pay 1.76% in real estate taxes or $5,280 per year. If you sold that home and bought a $300,000 home in South Carolina, you would pay 0.50% or $1,500 per year. That's a savings of $3,780 per year.

One couple sold their house in California because they were paying exorbitant real estate taxes. They wanted to simplify their lives during retirement. So, they put all their furniture and personal property in their garage, opened their garage door, knocked on their neighbors doors and told them to take what ever they wanted for free. Needless to say, their stuff was gone in no time and their neighbors were thrilled!

Next they bought a motor home to travel around the U.S. and then set up a mailbox in South Dakota. Not only did they eliminate real estate taxes, they also reduced their state income taxes. This couple travels around the country helping charities and visit family and friends. They found a fun, family-centered way to enjoy their retirement years.

Later in the book we'll discuss the concept of the three circles of finance more in depth, in which all the assets you own fit into one of three overlapping circles, labeled taxable, tax deferred, and tax free. By organizing all your investments in the three circles, you can better visualize how you may want to manage your investments to get additional tax advantages. By moving money from the taxable circle to the tax-deferred or tax-free circle, you are positioning your money to keep your taxes as low as possible.

CHAPTER 4

ROADBLOCK #3—
OLD-AGE ILLNESSES

HOW WELL ARE YOUR FINANCES?

Since the early 2000s, the financial security company Genworth has conducted the Cost of Care Survey, which collects data from more than 14,800 long-term care providers in 440 regions across the United States.

An application developed along with the survey allows you to pull down the cost of long-term care in your area or your region. The app uses the maps application on your smartphone to pinpoint your location and then displays the average cost of adult day care, at-home care, assisted living care, and skilled nursing care.

For example, in a few easy steps, I can see that in La Crosse, Wisconsin, where I'm located, the yearly rates for various types of long-term care on the date I used the application were: a home health aide at $49,142 for 44 hours per week; adult day care at $15,288 for five days per week; assisted living in a private, one-bedroom assisted living facility at $30,000; and a semi-private room in a skilled care facility, otherwise known as a nursing home, at $82,855. The app also calculates future years by assuming an annual growth rate of 3 percent.

Those costs are staggering.

And I'll repeat what I said earlier; no plan is still a plan. In other words, if you don't have a plan for covering these costs, your plan is that you're going to self-fund your long-term care costs.

If you do have a plan, what is it? Are you planning to give your home away to your kids? If you're planning to gift an asset to your children, have you sanitized it from capital gains tax? Depending on your plan, there may be tax issues you have yet to address.

Whatever your plan, the bottom line is that you will likely face the high cost of long-term care in your lifetime.

According to the Social Security Administration's life-expectancy calculator, the average 65-year-old man will live approximately 20 more years. If the average lifespan is 84, then a good percentage of people will live well into their 90s.

People are living longer, and as you get older it's inevitable that your body falls apart. It just doesn't function like it once did. The care we receive at the end of our lives is very expensive, and there needs to be a plan in place to deal with the expenses you'll likely face.

THE GOOD NEWS

There is good news for people today under the Pension Protection Act of 2006; you can now move money from an old CD that may have been making .5 percent, and you might get an improved rate of return.

For example, from a case study in the book *Don't Go Broke in a Nursing Home*, by Don Quante, if Mary puts $50,000 from her CDs into an asset-based long-term care policy, she may get over

$200,000 of tax-free long-term care benefits from that $50,000 investment. If Mary never went into a long-term care facility and died, then her heirs would receive over $100,000 tax-free as a death benefit from a $50,000 investment. In summary, Mary may be able to quadruple her investment for long-term care benefits. If she doesn't use her long-term care insurance, her heirs may receive double what she invested upon her death. That's a four-to-one or two-to-one leverage. Not bad for a safer investment strategy!

MARY: ASSET PRESERVATION STRATEGY COMBO LIFE & LTC

Based on a 65-year-old female non-smoker in good health

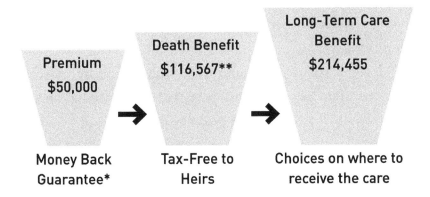

| Premium $50,000 | → | Death Benefit $116,567** | → | Long-Term Care Benefit $214,455 |
| Money Back Guarantee* | | Tax-Free to Heirs | | Choices on where to receive the care |

* Return of premium products are limited. Please consult an insurance agent for more information. ** 116,567 at age 65 varies by carrier. Income tax free according to current tax code. Life insurance guarantees rely on the financial strength and claims-paying ability of the issuing insurer. These examples are hypothetical, and are not intended to provide a rec-ommendation for any specific financial product, nor is this information intended to be used as the sole basis for financial decisions, nor should it be construed as advice designed to meet the particular needs of an individual's situation.

There are a number of other strategies today that may help investors protect their assets from the costs of long-term care. For example, if Bill is a veteran of a defined war, he may qualify for monthly aid for himself and his spouse. Or, as a last resort, in some instances it's actually possible to use Medicaid to pay for long-term care and still protect assets.

Still, you need to be prepared for whatever happens in your old age.

My father had life threatening illnesses when he was nearly 80 years old. At that age, he discovered that recovery was filled with complications and took longer than when he was younger. After struggling with infections and a near death experience, he recovered and is now thanking God for his health at age 87.

During his rehab experience, he had to see a physical therapist at a skilled nursing care facility. This was covered for only 100 days through his Medicare policy and after that he was on his own, (See Medicare.gov).

Unfortunately, fewer insurance companies are offering long-term care insurance, and those that do offer it are upping their premiums as much as 80 percent.

That happened to a friend of mine. After his premiums went up by 50 percent, he visited his financial advisor and expressed concern that his premiums would rise again dramatically the following year. So his advisor set up a trust to help protect his money. He still keeps his IRA money to live on, but the money he transfers into the asset protection trust is available to him and to his spouse through income rights while they're alive.

Today, families around the world care for folks in their old age; multiple generations of family live in one house. How do they do it in developing economies? Is that where we're going in the United States, with multiple generations living together in one residence?

You do have a long-term care plan today, either by design or by default. Do you really want to fail to plan in this area and become dependent on your family or friends to care for you? There are things you can do like ownership changes, asset-protection trusts, asset-based long-term care policies, or other traditional plans. Talk to your wealth advisor today to help you make plans to keep together what you've worked so hard to put together.

CHAPTER 4 TAKEAWAYS:

RESULTS FROM GENWORTH'S 2014 COST OF CARE STUDY:

		MINIMUM	RATE RANGE MEDIAN	MAXIMUM	MEDIAN ANNUAL RATE	FIVE-YEAR ANNUAL GROWTH
HOME	Homemaker Services Hourly Rates	$15	$21	$32	**$46,904**	2%
	Home Health Aide Services Hourly Rates	$17	$22	$32	**$50,336**	1%
COMMUNITY	Adult Day Health Care Daily Rates	$36	$60	$100	**$15,600**	2%
FACILITY	Assisted Living Facility (One Bedroom - Single Occupancy) Monthly Rates	$911	$3,850	$9,750	**$46,200**	4%
	Nursing Home (Semi Private Room) Daily Rates	$170	$239	$516	**$87,363**	4%
	Nursing Home (Private Room) Daily Rates	$195	$267	$516	**$97,455**	4%

Source: https://www.genworth.com/dam/Americas/US/PDFs/Consumer/
corporate/130568_032514_CostofCare_FINAL_nonsecure.pdf

AVERAGE COST OF ASSISTED LIVING EXPENSES:

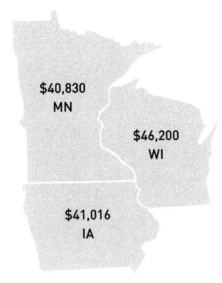

AVERAGE COST FOR SEMI-PRIVATE ROOM IN
A SKILLED NURSING CARE FACILITY:

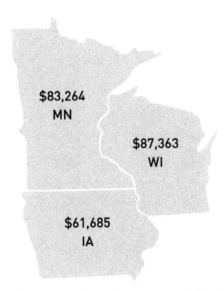

Source: https://www.genworth.com/dam/Americas/US/PDFs/Consumer/
corporate/130568_032514_CostofCare_FINAL_nonsecure.pdf

ROADBLOCK #4—PROCRASTINATION

IS IT REALLY TOO LATE?

Procrastination is another roadblock that keeps people from being financially secure.

If you're someone who's struggling with this roadblock, it's likely that retirement seemed a long way off when you were in your 20s. It was so far off, it seemed like it wasn't even you that was going to retire—like it was someone else's concern. So you spent all your earnings on cars, big toys, living expenses, and so on.

Then all of a sudden you were 30, and maybe you were married, had children, or were buying a house. All of these pieces of life kept you from saving for retirement. By your 40s, the kids were going to college or in need of other kinds of financial support.

In your 50s, you're ten years from retirement, so you throw your hands up and think the effort is futile. And in your 60s, you just decide your only option is to work forever.

But now is not the time to think about what there isn't; now is the time to think about what you can do with what there is.

If you were to talk to a coworker who wanted to help you financially, he or she would say get started now; save 15 percent and put it in growth stocks right now and do it the rest of your life. People who payroll deduct and put the money in growth investments, and do that in a slow, steady, methodical way for 20, 30, or 40 years, retire with more assets than the people who didn't invest over the long term.

So start today to do what you can, and don't put it off. You don't know the number of your days.

BASICS OVER TIME

Even if you're beyond your early investment years, it's not too late to do something now and to share your wisdom with younger generations.

Those younger generations should put as much money as possible in growth investments, such as stocks, exchange-traded funds, or mutual funds, according to their risk tolerance.

When you get to at least five years from retirement, you should begin putting the landing gear down. Begin by assessing your postretirement risk tolerance, and then gradually move from your current risk tolerance to your postretirement risk tolerance.

For example, if you are currently a growth investor with about 80 percent invested in stocks and your postretirement risk tolerance comes out at a maximum of 60 percent in stocks, that's a 20 percent difference. If you divide that 20 percent by five years, that's 4 percent per year to move out of stocks and into bonds or a fixed account within your investment accounts.

Let's assume you are 62 and you want to retire in five years at 67. If you are now a growth investor with 80 percent in stocks, you will subtract 4 percent every year from age 62 through age 66 so that you end up with only 60 percent invested in stocks at age 67.

AGE	62	63	64	65	66	67
STOCKS	80%	76%	72%	68%	64%	60%
BONDS	20%	24%	28%	32%	36%	40%

The above chart is meant to guide you smoothly from your preretirement asset allocation to your postretirement asset allocation. It is not meant to tell you what your risk tolerance is. To determine your risk tolerance you take a risk tolerance test, and that score will help guide you to a customized portfolio suitable to your risk tolerance. I suggest that you notch down your postretirement risk tolerance between 20 percent and 40 percent less than you set it during your working years.

Why? If you experience losses early in your retirement years, you might not make those losses back. Keep in mind that you might be withdrawing funds every month to live on. This creates a strain on your portfolio that you may not be able to recover from. Start more conservatively early in your retirement, and then, if you feel the need to take more risk, do it a few years or more after your retirement date.

Ideally, you want the stock market to be low while you're investing every month in your 401(k) plan. Five years before retirement, you want the market to spike to the highest point it's ever been to. At that point, you should take some of those gains off the table and diversify them to safe-money strategies. Also consider putting investment seat belts and air bags on some of your stock investments. You may want to explore AssetLock as one of those seat belts. We'll discuss investment seat belts and air bags in greater detail later in the book.

ON THE FLIP SIDE

Conversely, how many people do you know who passed away sooner than they expected? You have to live your life along the way, too.

When I first started in this business in my early 20s, some of my clients told me to go travel and enjoy myself while I was young and healthy because when I grew older I might not be able to get around as well. John Wesley said that you should "make all you can, save all you can, and give all you can." I would also like to add…spend all you can.

So in addition to not procrastinating financially, don't procrastinate when it comes to enjoying the journey of life. This is all about being present in life, making sure you're taking care of your budget and your emergency funds, being with the people you love, taking a little time to have fun, and then sharing your blessings with others.

Now maybe you're saying, "But Brent, I can't do it all."

If that's how you feel, then maybe it's time to consider your standard of living. One of the greatest assets some of my clients have is the ability to live below their means; that helps them live a more balanced life along the way as they save money.

So should you sell your house and move into a smaller place when your home is the one thing you truly value and enjoy? Really, it all depends on what you value.

What I'm saying is that you should live your life, but don't neglect to save money along the way, or you will regret it. Enjoy your life when you're younger; enjoy traveling, enjoy your kids. Have fun with friends and family. But don't make the mistake of climbing the ladder of success only to find that the ladder's leaning against the wrong building. No one lying on their deathbed ever said they wished they had spent more time at the office.

"So teach us to number our days, that we may present to You a heart of wisdom" (Psalms 90:12). It's about having the right perspective, doing what you can do today, taking it one step at a time, and living one day at a time.

If procrastination is one of your roadblocks, instead of beating yourself up, take time to reflect on what you've done right in life: Where are you doing with your personal, professional, and financial life? Look at ways to balance these three areas of your life so that you can live it to the fullest with yourself, your family and friends, and your community.

CHAPTER 5 TAKEAWAYS:

DON'T PROCRASTINATE! TIME IS ON YOUR SIDE!

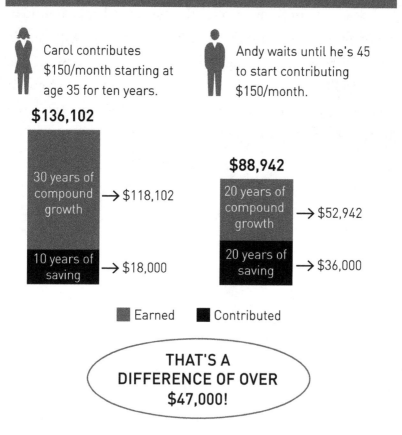

SAVE $150/MONTH – EARN 8% PER YEAR

Carol contributes $150/month starting at age 35 for ten years.

Andy waits until he's 45 to start contributing $150/month.

$136,102

30 years of compound growth → $118,102

10 years of saving → $18,000

$88,942

20 years of compound growth → $52,942

20 years of saving → $36,000

■ Earned   ■ Contributed

THAT'S A DIFFERENCE OF OVER $47,000!

Hypothetical assumption—not based on any specific investment alternative. Plan returns will vary and are not guaranteed. Both Carol and Andy invest $150 per month, but Carol starts ten years earlier and invests half as much and ends up with over 50 percent more money because she didn't procrastinate.

Source: Ameritas 401(k) enrollment power point 2014.

CHAPTER *6*

ROADBLOCK #5—RUNNING OUT OF MONEY

DO YOU REALLY HAVE ENOUGH TO LAST?

Most of us have probably known a relative or friend who had a pension plan; they'd retire, perhaps with a gold watch, and then the company would take care of them until the end of their days. They traded a lifetime of work with that company for the privilege of being taken care of forever.

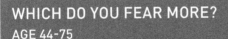

WHICH DO YOU FEAR MORE?
AGE 44-75

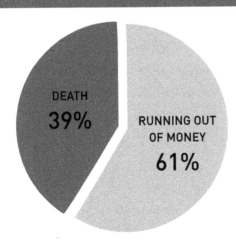

DEATH
39%

RUNNING OUT
OF MONEY
61%

Today, workers don't get taken care of for the rest of their lives. The companies that have guaranteed pension plans are fewer, and the markets, the economy, and the world are precarious. We live in a world where people, essentially, are afraid of living too long: Allianz' 2010 "Reclaiming the Future" study found that people ages 44–75 are more afraid of outliving their money than of dying.

Because of underperforming investing, an unstable economy, and a volatile stock market, today's pension plans have become too difficult to fund, and burgeoning, unfunded pension liabilities have grown unmanageable. The Pension Benefit Guaranty Corporation (PBGC), a federal agency created by the Employee Retirement Income Security Act of 1974 (ERISA) to protect pension benefits in the private sector, is essentially broke. According to the PBGC 2014 annual report[1]:

> As of September 30, 2014, the single-employer and multiemployer programs reported deficits of $19,338 million and $42,434 million, respectively. The multiemployer program's net position declined by $34,176 million, increasing its deficit to $42,434 million, an all-time record high for the multiemployer program.
>
> Notwithstanding these deficits, the Corporation has about $88,013 million in single-employer assets and $1,769 million in multiemployer assets and will be able to meet its obligations for a number of years. However, neither program at present has the resources to fully satisfy PBGC's obligations in future years.

---

1   "Annual Report," Pension Benefit Guarantee Corporation, 2014, http://www.pbgc.gov/documents/2014-annual-report.pdf#page=23.

In short, the PBGC can't even afford to insure the pensions that it has. If there were a run on the bank, it couldn't afford to keep the pensions together.

So we have a corporate world in America that decided to put the burden of retirement back on the individual employee by creating defined contribution plans, such as 401(k) or profit sharing/money purchase pension plans, 403(b) plans, and 457 deferred compensation plans.

The illusion is that we retire with hundreds of thousands of dollars, if not millions of dollars, in a retirement plan and think that having that big pile of money means we're secure. We've never had control of that kind of money before.

The reality is that we still make money in one of two ways: People at work or money at work. When we're not at work anymore, we need our money to be at work for us to give us a paycheck every month. If our money is 100 percent invested in the bank, then we can't earn enough interest to pay ourselves a big enough paycheck to live on. If we invest all our money in bonds, rising interest rates might cause the bond value to fall, leaving us without enough income to live on; we certainly are not going to have an inflation hedge with a 100 percent bond portfolio. If we invest it all in the stock market, we might face up to two 50 percent losses within the next decade, according to John Bogle from Vanguard.

So if that's the case with these investment strategies, what do we do? There's no hope, right? Looking at the different options, you can't put it all in the bank and expect to get a decent return. Bonds are moving into a bear market, and the stock market roller coaster is now moving at a nauseating pace. You can't necessarily put all your money in gold anymore. You can't necessarily put it in real estate either, because most people can't manage a real estate portfolio—they don't know how to fix the hinges on doors or do plumbing, electrical work, or any of the manual tasks involved.

So what does a person do? I believe this; you need to create a diversified portfolio by using the Eight Investment Strategies for Life, which we'll talk more about in the chapters ahead.

The old strategies, like putting all your money in a stock mutual fund or in a bond fund or in the bank, don't seem to work anymore. All these things have to work together with new strategies that you may not be aware of.

COVARIANCE IS KEY

The key is to create a portfolio of covariance, which is a situation in which two waves go in opposite directions. For example, if you have two roller coasters superimposed, when one is at the top of the hill, the other is at the bottom of the trough, and vice versa.

When you use covariance with value stocks and growth stocks—when you invest in them together—you may experience a relatively smoother ride. When you have stocks versus bonds versus commodities versus cash, and you have them in different percentages, you can create some covariance protection when the stock market goes down. Whether the stock market goes up or down, interest rates rise or fall or commodities surge or plummet, covariance can help give you a smoother ride.

Essentially, it's about not putting all your eggs in one basket.

Let me draw you a picture.

My dad grew up on a farm where they had an apple orchard and grew strawberries, and they had 6,000 laying hens.

One day when he was in high school, he was practicing his trumpet in the kitchen. But the noise drove his mother crazy, so she told him to go practice outside. Well, he went out to the chicken coop and practiced there, and, as a result, all 6,000 hens molted and were unable to lay eggs. Their systems were shocked, and for 90 days the farm was out of the egg business.

In fact, it essentially destroyed the family's egg business. Without a steady supply of eggs, they ended up selling the chickens, because, well, let's face it, all of their eggs were in one basket.

Fortunately, my grandparents were able to convert their farm into a housing development and then start a lumber yard and component home manufacturing business called CBS Homes. The Minnesota Chamber of Commerce named my grandparent's and parent's business runner up for business of the year in the late 1970's, second only to Totino's Pizza Co.

That's where Solomon's wisdom rings true. He invested in silver and gold and traded in perfumes and spices, real estate, and livestock. He had a fleet of ships, thousands of sheep and goats, and I suppose cattle. He had a fleet of ships, thousands of employees, servants and abundant livestock. He owned vast real estate holdings. He was a trader of thoroughbred horses and spices and gold and silver. He was a billionaire by todays standards because of his wise business decisions. The Lord had blessed him indeed. His wise investments were diversified and he experienced the benefits of covariance.

CHAPTER 6 TAKEAWAYS:

COVARIANCE

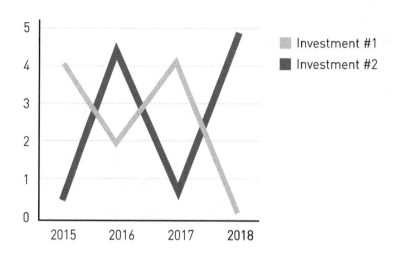

Covariance is when two investments act in opposite correlation. This is a hypothetical graph for illustration purposes only. No investments act perfectly or predictably or in perfectly opposite correlation. That's why we recommend that you consider deciding which investments you may like to use from the following Retirement Pyramid.

THE RETIREMENT PYRAMID: "WE GUIDE, YOU DECIDE."

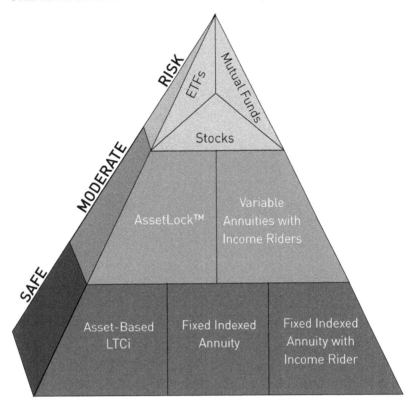

CHAPTER 7

ROADBLOCK #6—
UNSTABLE ECONOMY

BURSTING BUBBLES

You don't have to think back in history too far to remember what it felt like to experience two economic bubbles burst in our economy. In the last decade and a half, you experienced the real estate bubble bursting and the stock market bubble popping as well. Real estate values around the United States dropped 22 to 50 percent. Real estate values in the Midwest seemed to drop around 30 percent, and in California, Arizona, Nevada, and Florida, real estate values dropped by up to 50 percent.

Since 1989, the stock market has seen three declines of approximately 50 percent. The tech bubble burst, then we had 9/11 followed by the banking crisis. Do you remember what you were doing or where you were when the Twin Towers were attacked by terrorists?

You also don't have to think back too far to remember when, without congressional intervention, US government bonds would have defaulted in what would have been the first ever government bond default in US history.

When economic bubbles burst and volatility takes over, we are all experiencing an unstable economy.

America's past is filled with challenges: famine, drought, the banking crisis, the stock market crash of 1929, the Dust Bowl, the Civil War, world wars, pandemics…all of these factors can create a very unstable economy.

Political unrest can also lead to an unstable economy. When political leaders don't work together as they should, when allied overseas governments topple or collapse, these are issues that create challenges for our economy.

What that means is your money may become as unstable as the economy.

Economic instability was a topic discussed by economist David Wiedemer and his brother Robert Wiedemer in their best-selling book, *Aftershock*, in which they outlined predictions of a series of economic bubbles that would burst and cause horrific trouble for the individual investor.

In line with their first prediction, the real estate bubble greatly affected investments, with property values plunging 22 to 50 percent in various areas of the United States from 2004 to 2014.

According to the Wiedemers, two bubbles remain, which may burst in the near future.

The first of these is the default of US Treasury bonds. If government bonds default, the United States will not be viewed as a safe haven for the global economy. Trust will be broken and the endless demand for purchasing our government debt may diminish. If we cannot continue to borrow our way out of our troubles, America may face very tough times.

The second overinflated bubble that may burst in the near future is the US dollar. If the dollar collapses, our money won't be worth the paper it's printed on. What will happen to your money if the US dollar collapses? Your stocks and equity mutual funds may drop in value because of the systemic risk of currencies and the stock market.

THE PRINTING PRESS

Warren Buffet said on CNBC back during the 2008 banking crisis that "As long as America has a printing press, we're fine." In other words, as long as we can print money, we can always pay off our debt. Okay, let's assume that tomorrow morning we print $18 trillion to pay off the debt, and we pay it all off, 100 percent. What happens to the dollars in your wallet or purse? That's right, the dollars you own will be worth substantially less, if anything.

Inflation may be the inherent result of printing money. You and I could also face stagflation because of printed money; that is, inflation with a stagnant economy. CNBC reported on September 25, 2013, that the Fed has a hidden agenda behind money-printing. Peter Tanous for CNBC said:

>...the Fed has accumulated an unprecedented balance sheet of more than $3.6 trillion, which needs to go somewhere, someday...

>I believe that one of the most important reasons the Fed is determined to keep interest rates low is one that is rarely talked about, and which comprises a dark economic foreboding that should frighten us all.

>Let me ask you a question: How would you feel if you knew that almost all of the money you pay in personal income tax went to pay just one bill, the interest on the

debt? Chances are, you and millions of Americans would
find that completely unacceptable and indeed they should.
But that is where we may be heading.

INTERESTING INTEREST RATES

Meanwhile, interest rates have been dropping since 1980 according to JP Morgan Asset Management in its Second-Quarter 2015 Fact Book. They peaked on September 13, 1981, at 15.84 percent for nominal ten-year treasury yields, according to JP Morgan Asset Management in its Third-Quarter 2014 Fact Book. While interest rates dropped from 15.84 percent in 1981 all the way down to 0.58 percent on June 30, 2012, they spiked up in the first quarter of 2013. As of this writing, they're currently at 2.17 percent.

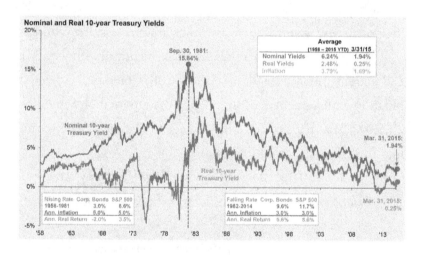

Source: 2nd Quarter 2015 JP Morgan Fact Book

In other words, over the course of 30 years we hit a low of a half percent before interest rates started rising in 2013 as bonds dropped in value.

What this demonstrates is that interest rates have an inverse relationship to bond values.

Picture a teeter-totter on the playground. As interest rates rise on one end of that teeter-totter, bond values drop on the other end.

What relevance does this have today? When Janet Yellen took office as the new chairperson of the Federal Reserve Board in 2014, she said, "We will continue to raise interest rates in the near future." Not long after that, the bond market had huge losses; her comment was a shot across the bow, a warning that bond values may continue to fall as interest rates continue to rise in the future.

The point is that bond investments may not yield what they did over the last 30 years. The bull market on bonds may be over, and we may be entering a bear market on bonds. That's part of our unstable economy.

During a tour of a local bank a decade ago, I learned about an interesting story of Winona, Minnesota's fascinating history. The King family used to own the Watkins Company in Winona, Minnesota. For the King family, 30-year, long-term US Treasuries were an exceptionally good investment from the early 1980s until somewhere around 2010. The returns the King family earned from government bonds were reportedly a little under 10 percent, rivaling the long-term returns of the stock market.

Much of the King family assets were held by a local bank that faced a dilemma of what to do when those 30-year US Treasuries matured. If the local bank decided to reinvest in, they would do so for just a fraction of what they were earning during the 30-year bond bull market. Therefore the bank needed to get back into the loan business and the retirement plan business.

Bloomberg Business reported on its website on January 20, 2015, that 30-year US Treasuries were paying 2.45 percent—not a good investment for the next 30 years. Later in this book, we explore alternatives to bonds, since the bull market on bonds may be over.

THE RISE AND FALL OF CIVILIZATIONS

Great Britain, Rome, Persia—there are numerous stories about the rise and fall of global economic powers in our world's history.

Recently, Greece overpromised its public employees fat pensions and no worries. However, because there were more checks going out than were coming in, Greek government pension benefits had to be cut. People rioted in the streets because the government couldn't afford to make payments as promised, and the nation went broke.

Is America next? Not if we work on putting together the human and capital resources to resolve what's missing in our country.

Let's not forget what's going right in America. One of history's brightest investors, the late Sir john Templeton, talked endlessly about the fact that we're living in the greatest time the world has seen. We have more scientists and more highly educated people, and our capacity utilization is greater, as is our productivity because of technology.

My life coach, Doug Carter, suggests that individuals look at their personal economy and ask not what went wrong but what is right. What's currently going well? What are you doing to make things right? What's ideally right? What's missing? What human and capital resources are needed to fulfill what's missing?

When you begin to ask those questions as a coach of a sports team, as a leader of a business or a church, or in your own personal life, you begin to become more aware of what's going right, and you begin to take inventory and treasure the blessings in your life so you develop more of an attitude of gratitude.

CHAPTER 7 TAKEAWAYS:

THE WHAT'S RIGHT CONVERSATION[2]

1. What's currently going right? _____

_____

_____

_____

2. What are you doing to make it right? _____

_____

_____

_____

3. What's ideally right? _____

_____

_____

_____

4. What's missing? _____

_____

_____

_____

5. What human and financial resources are needed to meet what's missing? _____

_____

_____

_____

_____

2   Source: Doug Carter, President, Carter Institue, Inc. clientsforever@ sbcglobal.net 1(530) 926-3782

CHAPTER 8

ROADBLOCK #7—INFLATION

WHAT'S THE RISK?

INFLATION – THE PRICE OF STAMPS

1953 POSTAGE

2015 POSTAGE

3¢   49¢

Source: http://about.usps.com/who-we-are/postal-history/domestic-letter-rates-since-1863.pdf

Since 1926, the average rate of inflation has been 3 percent. In 1953, the cost of a first-class postage stamp was $0.03. Today, it costs $0.49 to mail a first-class letter. In 1953, the price of a gallon of gasoline was $0.10, and today that same gallon of gas is $2.46 per gallon. Now, let me ask you a question: Did the car you most recently purchased cost more that the first house you bought? If so, that is a good example of inflation.

If you use the rule of 72 divided by the interest rate, you get the number of years it takes to double your money. For example, if you take 72 and divide it by the interest rate of 3 percent, you find that it takes 24 years to double your money. Inversely, at 3 percent inflation your dollar is worth fifty cents in 24 years.

Translate this to your balance sheet. If you retire at age 66, then in 24 years you are age 90. If your age 66 postretirement income needs are $50,000 per year, then your income needs at age 90 may be $100,000 per year to keep pace with inflation.

SOCIAL INSECURITY – WHAT YOUR SS STATEMENT SAYS:

Without changes, in 2033 the Social Security Trust Fund will be able to pay only about 75 cents for each dollar of scheduled benefits.

Although Social Security is adjusted for inflation, by 2033 recipients may only be getting $0.75 on the dollar in benefits. If you read the fine print on your most recent benefit statement on the administration's website, ssa.gov, it goes on to say, "We need to resolve these issues soon to make sure Social Security continues to provide a foundation of protection for future generations."

Pretend you have a printing press in your garage and you can print all the money you want to pay your bills; that's what our government does. Wouldn't you overspend every year, since you simply have to print more money to spend it? That's precisely what the Fed is doing. When the Federal Reserve Board uses tools like "quantitative easing" to issue government bonds for the Fed's balance sheet and purchases them with printed money, it also affects how the US dollar correlates with currencies around the world. The current logic seems to be that a "rising tide lifts all the boats."

We live in a society that operates on what's called "fiat currency," in which everything is based on the value of paper money or coins. There's really no value to the money that we have—the value is kind of an illusion. It's created and it's maintained by all the global systems. It's propped up by banks that are guaranteed by the Federal Deposit Insurance Corporation (FDIC), which is just a promise to pay.

So what does this mean to you and your money? You can't just put your head in the sand and pretend none of it's going on and not change what you're doing. But you also can't sit around in a straightjacket of worry bouncing off the padded walls of your house.

So what can you do?

Invest wisely in things that guarantee your income, that keep pace with inflation, and that protect your downside risk in the investment world. These are all part of the Eight Investment Strategies for Life.

What are the factors that keep inflation in check? Well, there are two sides to that equation. There are the things you can't control—how much debt the Federal Reserve takes on, how much money the Congressional Budget Office (CBO) prints, the price of gasoline—and the things that you can control, which is the way you diversify your investments.

TWO TYPES OF INVESTMENTS

There are really only two types of investments: ownership and loanership. Loanership investments are those in which you loan dollars to somebody else and earn an interest rate on but have no equity growth in. These include bank accounts, such as money markets, checking accounts, and bond investments that pay you interest but no capital gains.

Ownership investments are those that you own and that pay you in the form of interest, dividends, or realized or unrealized capital gains.

For example, would you rather put your money in the bank or would you rather own the bank? If you put money in the bank you earn interest. But if you own the bank, you're earning all the profits on everybody else's money that's in the bank on interest.

Ownership dollars should not be absent from your portfolio. That's one of the only inflation hedges left.

For example, real estate has appreciation. If you own a duplex valued at $240,000, and on each side of the duplex you charge $1,000 a month for rent, that would be $2,000 a month total. That's $24,000 a year of 10 percent gross income, minus all your expenses. Maybe you'll net 6 or 7 percent, but that's still pretty good interest. Plus, the value of the real estate over a period of 10 to 20 years typically goes up 1 to 3 percent. That's an inflation hedge.

You can also keep the income you generate from these properties in pace with inflation because your rents naturally go up with inflation. That's an inflation hedge. It's also an equity investment, which is an ownership dollar.

Even if you don't want the headaches of owning real estate, you could own a real estate investment trust through a stock or a mutual fund.

Another form of ownership dollars are publically traded stocks. Dividend-paying stocks may continue paying you a dividend even if the markets are volatile. Let's say that you believed electricity was going to be in big demand even during tough times. You may experience some stability in this type of investment. You have an opportunity to profit directly from the profits of a utility company. That's another form of equity ownership.

One 92-year-old woman confided in me before she died that a few decades ago she and her husband wanted to buy curtains in their house but decided to put money in a bank stock instead. About 20 years later, the $2,000 investment in a local private bank stock was worth $200,000.

Stocks and real estate investments may help you keep pace with inflation since they are considered an equity investment. Equity investments in the stock market have averaged over 10% while inflation has averaged over 3% since 1926 according to Ibbotson & Associates Stocks, Bonds, Bills and Inflation chart. Because you may be able to earn more than inflation over time, an inflation hedge can be created.

CHAPTER 8 TAKEAWAYS

INFLATION AS MEASURED BY THE CPI—
CONSUMER PRICE INDEX

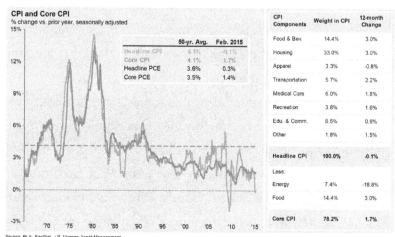

CPI and Core CPI
% change vs. prior year, seasonally adjusted

	50-yr. Avg.	Feb. 2015
Headline CPI	4.1%	-0.1%
Core CPI	4.1%	1.7%
Headline PCE	3.6%	0.3%
Core PCE	3.5%	1.4%

CPI Components	Weight in CPI	12-month Change
Food & Bev.	14.4%	3.0%
Housing	33.0%	3.0%
Apparel	3.3%	-0.8%
Transportation	5.7%	2.2%
Medical Care	6.0%	1.8%
Recreation	3.8%	1.6%
Edu. & Comm.	6.5%	0.8%
Other	1.8%	1.5%
Headline CPI	**100.0%**	**-0.1%**
Less:		
Energy	7.4%	-18.8%
Food	14.4%	3.0%
Core CPI	**78.2%**	**1.7%**

Source: BLS, FactSet, J.P. Morgan Asset Management.
CPI used is CPI-U and values shown are % change vs. one year ago and reflect February 2015 CPI data. CPI component weights are as of February 2015.
Core CPI is defined as CPI excluding food and energy prices. The Personal Consumption Expenditure (PCE) deflator employs an evolving chain-weighted basket of consumer expenditures instead of the fixed weight basket used in CPI calculations.
Data are as of March 31, 2015.

CHAPTER 9

ROADBLOCK #8—NO PLAN

A COSTLY STRATEGY

Usually when you visit with your doctor, he or she examines your physical condition or areas of concern to determine what ails you. That exam precedes the recommendation and the prescription.

In the financial world, it's just as essential to get an examination first, before getting a prescription. A financial physical organizes your current investments, estate plans, retirement plans, and asset protection plans, and then pinpoints areas to help you get back on track.

Recommendations may be part of your financial physical. You could reject them all, choose a few to implement, or implement all of them. You can implement them all yourself, with someone else's help, or with the help of a retirement wealth advisor.

While a visit to the doctor often comes with a cost, putting off a visit when you have a need sometimes leads to even greater costs. It's the same with your financial health: there's a cost for doing something, and there's a cost for doing nothing, and quite often doing nothing costs much more.

The cost of putting together a financial plan may be around a tenth of 1 percent of your investable assets. For example, if you have $500,000 of assets to invest, your plan may cost you approximately $500 to put together.

My question to you is this: Is there value in the $500 you spend with your retirement wealth advisor? That $500 may save you as much or even more in taxes. For that small fee, you may be able to protect your assets from the high cost of long-term care or avoid probate costs. Any one of the strategies or ideas you implement may save you considerably more than the $500 you spent on the plan. In my opinion, getting a financial physical is extremely important if you want to know whether or not you are on track for a successful retirement.

The cost of doing nothing can be assessed in many ways. One of those ways is by looking at how your investments are structured. If you have all of your money in the lowest-cost index strategy, you may be very happy, since you're paying only one quarter of 1 percent to manage your money.

At first glance, this seems to be the least expensive option for you. However, if the stock market loses 50 percent and your investments also lose 50 percent, isn't the low cost of the management dwarfed by the 50 percent loss due to lack of management?

Justice Learned Hand said,

"Anyone may arrange his affairs so that his taxes shall be as low as possible; he is not bound to choose that pattern which best pays the treasury. There is not even a patriotic duty to increase one's taxes…Nobody owes any public duty to pay more than the law demands."

Read more at http://www.westernjournalism.com/august-18-judge-learned-hand/#7gpicdmTSGLbwjQO.9

In the estate planning world, there is a huge cost for doing nothing. In America, there is a tax for dieing. The top federal estate tax of 40% begins at estates valued just over $5.43 million per person, source: forbes.com. Each state has a unique estate tax rate as well. For example, the death tax rate begins with estates of $1.4 million in 2015 and increases by $200k every year until it reaches $2 million in 2018. The death tax rate can be 10% to 15% per spouse, source: house.leg.state.mn.us.

In the case of the Rockefellers, the difference was a whopping 48 percent of the estate. The father didn't have an astute estate plan, so he lost 64 percent to the IRS, whereas the son learned how to protect assets and use more advanced strategies, and he lost only 16 percent of the estate to the government.

To reiterate, quite often the cost of being informed is a lot less than being uninformed.

THE MONEY GAME

Would you buy the cheapest parachute to use in jumping out of an airplane? Would you buy the cheapest fire extinguisher available? Or, if you're jumping off the Golden Gate Bridge with a bungee cord attached to you, do you want the least expensive bungee cord? The lowest price is not always what you want. Sometimes you want the most protection or the highest quality, and higher quality often comes with a higher price.

The cost of doing nothing with your investments other than, for example, putting them in a low-cost index fund may be very high. If your concern as you approach retirement or during your retirement years is preservation of capital, then you may want your advisor to move some of your money out of the market at the right time. An active money management strategy may cost a little bit more in management fees, but the fee you pay for active management may help you protect your assets at a time when you are worried about your financial future.

The reality of the market is that, if you lose 50 percent in the market in any given year, you have to make 100 percent just to get back to even.

Try playing the money game with me: Start with $2, and let's say that Mr. Market gives you a 50 percent return. That would add four quarters or another dollar to your pile of money. Now you have $3.

Now if Mr. Market takes away 50 percent of what you have, that's $1.50. So take $1.50 from your pile of $3.00 and you are left with $1.50.

You started with $2 and by adding $1, you made 50 percent. But when you lose 50 percent, you lose $1.50. That is a loss of 25 percent of your original investment. A mutual fund prospectus may say that a gain of 50 percent and a loss of 50 percent is a net gain of 0 percent. However, if the average rate of return was 0 percent after being up 50 percent one year and down 50 percent the next, then your losses were 25 percent—not 0 percent.

That's a high cost for doing nothing, in my opinion.

The Money Game concept was used with permission from the book *Stress-Free Retirement* by Patrick Kelly.

THE COST FOR PLANNING

Remember the story about my dad practicing his trumpet and destroying a 6,000-hen laying operation? That's the price of not diversifying a portfolio. The cost for not having an investment plan could be that your risk tolerance won't be achieved.

A friend of mine from high school did not have a plan. Her husband died young, leaving her with three young children and no insurance money. My friend had to go back to school to get a degree to earn a living, and she had to move back in with her parents so that they could watch the kids while she was in school. She eventually graduated from college, rented a place for her and the kids, and now her kids are grown and on their own.

But had her husband made a plan to take care of their financial affairs by funding it with life insurance, then when he died too soon that life insurance would have taken a lot of pressure off the family, because his widow would have had the resources she needed to take care of herself and her children on her own. In that case, the cost of not planning was devastating to the surviving spouse.

This story is one of many that illustrate what's really important; it's important to lay out strategies that will take care of your family in the event you live too long, die too soon, or become disabled along the way. Those are part of the foundation of the plan that you need to build.

APPROPRIATE PLANNING

Any plan should meet your values, ideals, goals, and objectives. If your advisor doesn't understand those, then the plan he or she builds is not going to be a plan that's custom-designed for you.

Everyone is different, so everyone should have a customized plan.

Take the case of the couple whose financial advisor told them that they needed to live on an income of under $32,000 to avoid paying taxes on their Social Security. What astonished me was that they had nearly $1 million in their retirement plan on top of Social Security. Their Social Security was around $30,000 per year.

They were hardly spending any of their money, because the financial planner told them that they could live their life without paying tax on any of their Social Security. When they came to see me and I asked them how much they'd like to live on, they said they'd like to live on about $4,000 per month but that they'd have to make $5,000 to live on the $4,000. After Social Security, they needed to pull out about $30,000 a year from their investments.

But, they told me, they felt they could do that if they pulled some of the interest out of their retirement plan and lived on their Social Security. "We feel like we could live on that $60,000 a year minus taxes and have all the things that we want, including travel," they said.

When I asked them why they didn't do that, it turned out they didn't realize it was an option. I told them, "You can do whatever you want to do. It's just that you'll need to pay tax on 85 percent of your Social Security." They didn't care. They just wanted to enjoy their life.

So with neither of them working, they spent the next year going on vacations and taking time to be with their kids and grandkids.

They had a great year together. Then, at the end of the year, the wife got terminal cancer and died within three months.

Later on, the husband told me that he was so thankful that we gave them permission to go live their life with freedom to spend the money that they'd worked so hard to put together. He said he never would have been able to have such a great year with his wife and really celebrate life if he had known in advance that his wife was going to pass away.

He said that loosening up his plan a little bit to enjoy life was the best advice he had been given.

So you need to have a plan. The lack of a plan can be costly in more ways than just financially. It can be emotionally costly, and it could also expose you to unwanted publicity. For example, if you didn't have a revocable living trust, your whole estate might be posted as public record at your county courthouse to be viewed by your entire community. Do you really want your private financial affairs to be posted as public record? Do you want to die without a plan? Don't fail to plan, and certainly don't plan to fail.

That concludes the eight roadblocks that may keep people from achieving financial freedom. Now we're going to discuss some solutions and strategies that are available to you; these strategies may add some value to your current retirement wealth plan. I call these the Eight Investment Strategies for Life.

CHAPTER 9 TAKEAWAYS:

 *THE EIGHT ROADBLOCKS TO FINANCIAL SECURITY AND PEACE (**STOP RUIN**)*

1. **S** Stock market losses
2. **T** Taxes
3. **O** Old-age illness
4. **P** Procrastination
5. **R** Running out of money
6. **U** Unstable economy
7. **I** Inflation
8. **N** No plan

INVESTMENT STRATEGY 1—STOCKS

ARE YOU READY FOR THE RIDE?

Earlier in the book, if you traveled back in time and visited with King Solomon using the time travel app on your smartphone, he might have advised you to invest your money in seven or eight different places, because you don't know what disasters may come. If you asked him, "What would be some of the Eight Investment Strategies for Life that would be appropriate for today?" King Solomon might have answered you by asking another question: "What disasters do you think you might face in the future?"

Now you have something to talk to him about. You just over-viewed the eight roadblocks to financial security and peace. You can remember these eight roadblocks with the acronym STOP RUIN: stock market losses, taxes, old-age illness, procrastination, running out of money, unstable economy, inflation, and no plan. Understanding the problem is the first step to finding the solution.

Now let's discuss the eight investment strategies or solutions that may help you overcome these roadblocks today.

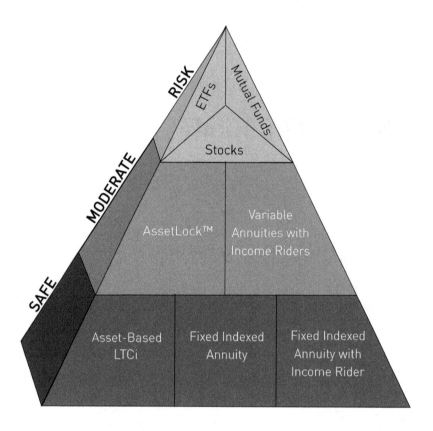

The next eight chapters of the book will address these strategies, starting with three high-risk strategies—individual stocks, exchange-traded funds (ETFs), and mutual funds—then two moderate-risk strategies—investment air bags (income riders on variable annuities) and AssetLock—and concluding with three safe strategies—upside potential without downside risk (fixed-index annuities or FIAs), taking guaranteed income for life (riders on FIAs), and old-age illness insurance (asset-based long-term care insurance or LTCi). The acronym I use to remember all this is SEMI-AUTO:

S   Stocks

E   ETFs

M   Mutual funds

I   Investment air bags

A   AssetLock or Welshire^{SM} Advance and Protect

U   Upside potential without downside risk

T   Taking guaranteed income for life

O   Old-age illness insurance

Talking with King Solomon, he would likely have started with the most basic investment of all, a stock investment, because that was a passion of his. Then he may have talked about the fleet of ships that he'd operated in joint venture with King Hiram: In 2 Chronicles 8:18, Hiram sent ships commanded by his own officers and manned by experienced sailors. These ships sailed to Ophir with Solomon's men and brought back to Solomon almost 17 tons of gold.

WHAT IS A STOCK?

Stocks are a type of ownership dollar, which we talked about earlier.

A stock is really a share in a company that has the opportunity to make money through dividends and growth in share value. Dividends are periodic payments made on stocks like utility companies or preferred stocks. Dividend-paying stocks seem to attract investors who want a more conservative stock investment. Growth is what you experience with a successful company whose stock price goes up from the price you paid for it. You can sell your shares and turn them into income whenever you want.

When you make a stock purchase, you actually own part of the company. For example, when you buy shares of Wal-Mart, you actually own the same shares of stock that the Walton family owns; this is the same stock that has made them billionaires, according to Forbes. The Walton family doesn't own a better form of shares than you do; they just have more of them.

As far as taxes are concerned, if you held the shares of the stock for years and years, you wouldn't pay tax on the unrealized capital gains until you sold that stock. Therefore, if there's appreciation in the value of those shares, you aren't taxed for that appreciation until those investments are sold. When they're sold, it's at a capital gains tax bracket, which is typically much lower than the ordinary income tax bracket.

HIGH-RISK STRATEGY

Don't forget that stocks are risky. A common disclaimer when investing in stocks warns that all investments have risk, including the loss of principal.

You don't have to think back too far to remember a company that went bankrupt and investors lost all their money. Enron, for example, was an investment-grade company that lost billions of dollars overnight for Enron stockholders.

There are risks with stocks that include business risk (for example, the risk of the company going broke) and market risk (the risk of the overall market that may not be attached to the earnings or valuation of the company). Market risk is a systemic risk and business risk is nonsystemic risk.

If the stock market is falling, then there are more sellers of investments than buyers, and the cost of your shares may be driven lower as well. This market risk is not necessarily contingent on the company profits; the price can go down while the value of the company is still intact.

A friend of mine, Jason Jenkins, creator of AssetLock, likes to ask two questions: "How much can you afford to lose on your investments?" and "How much are you willing to lose on your investments?" Once we get the answer to these questions, we can actually set a downside risk limit. This may help you create a backstop for your investments that may help you limit downside risk.

Stock market losses are on people's minds because we just went through the second greatest stock market crash since 1929, and because the market, historically, is just so erratic. To have all your money in the stock market is an emotional roller coaster during retirement. That's why we recommend having some of your money in safe investments and some in moderate investments, and more aggressive investors can keep the balance in risk-based investments.

ROADBLOCKS AVOIDED

Stocks are valuable for keeping pace with inflation, which we talked about as a roadblock to planning.

When you have stock market investments, you have one of the few places where historically you would have beat inflation two-to-one since 1926, according to Ibbotson Associates. Their famous chart, called "Stocks, Bonds, Bills, and Inflation," states that, since 1926, small company stocks have averaged 12.3 percent, large company stocks have averaged 10.1 percent, bonds have averaged just over 5 percent, and inflation has averaged 3 percent.

The point is that you might be able to keep pace with inflation if you invest some of your money in an asset class that historically beats inflation. That's one of the roadblocks that stocks may help you overcome. You may also keep your taxes lower, overcoming the taxes roadblock, because your stock investment is tax deferred for as long as you hold it. You can harvest out your tax gains efficiently by selling two stocks at once, one with a gain and one with a loss. Sell only that number of stock shares you need in order to generate the income you need to live on, and leave the rest of it to grow tax deferred.

You may overcome stock market losses by investing in growth stocks or in dividend-paying stocks. So, for example, even during the flat decade of the 1970s, you may have still been able to make a little dividend income if you owned dividend-paying stocks.

The Dow Jones Industrial Average opened around 800 in 1964 and closed around 800, 18 years later in 1982.

Stock income may be paid by the issuing company monthly, quarterly, or annually. The dividend typically is expressed in a yield percentage. For example, a stock trading at $20 with a $1 dividend per share would have a dividend yield of 5 percent.

Additionally, high-yielding dividend-paying stocks have outperformed general markets. According to Morningstar's March 1, 2013 report, stocks that pay dividends had a compound annual return of 9 percent compared with 5 percent for non-dividend-paying stocks during the period studied.

For the running out of money roadblock, dividend-paying stocks may help provide income for the rest of your life. Be aware, however, that there are no guarantees: those dividends are declared by the board of directors, and the company's decision to pay that dividend could change from year to year.

Dividend-paying stocks can help provide income during an unstable economy. Just look at those that earned money even through the Great Depression, seemingly ignoring the economic chaos of the stock market crash of 1929. Some of these companies are still around today: American Telephone and Telegraph (AT&T), Caterpillar Tractor, Chesapeake (Energy) Corp., Coca-Cola, Commonwealth Edison, General Foods, International Business Machines (IBM), and Kimberly-Clark Corporation.

Let's just think about today. What types of stocks might do well even in the most difficult times? Think about some of the products you would still buy even if you didn't have much money. You'd probably still buy canned soap and toilet paper, and you'd probably still buy electricity, fuel for your car, and toothpaste. It would seem that companies like Campbell Soup, Colgate Palmolive,

THE following compilation discloses some of the more important corporations which have ignored the recession and reported substantially higher profits in the first half of 1930 than in the corresponding period of 1929:

COMPANY	Net Income 1st Half 1930	1st Half 1929	% Increase 1st Half 1930 Over 1st Half 1929
Addressograph Int'l..	$781,471	$757,237	3.5
Air Reduction Co....	2,883,8+5	2,730,334	5.6
Allis-Chalmers	2,351,540	2,179,088	8.0
America Corporation	401,060	354,115	13.2
American Bank Note	1,461,648	1,460,088	0.1
Amer. Chain Co.....	1,185,216	1,034,029	14.6
Amer. Chicle Co.....	1,081,334	1,039,167	4.1
Amer. Tel. & Tel. Co.	81,671,847	80,102,039	2.0
Amer. Writing Paper	248,512	235,180	5.7
Anchor Cap Corp...	575,135	495,636	16.1
Autostrop Safety Razor	722,808	370,655	68.1
Bangor & Aroos. R. R.	1,300,056	916,549	41.9
Blaw-Knox Co.	1,684,002	1,392,366	20.9
Briggs Mfg. Co...	3,531,803	2,422,697	45.7
Bush Terminal Co...	743,511	686,264	8.4
Caterpillar Tractor..	5,622,965	5,279,431	6.5
Chesapeake Corp.	2,961,189	1,869,863	58.3
Childs Co.	668,328	420,342	59.0
Cluett, Peabody & Co.	418,041	332,841	25.5
Coca Cola	7,181,812	*6,491,904	10.7
Colo. Fuel and Iron..	1,619,053	1,419,453	14.1
Commercial Invest. Tr.	4,738,684	4,042,116	17.2
Commonwealth Edison	8,785,666	8,446,157	3.8
Consolidated Laundries	386,656	325,132	18.9
Container Corp. of Am.	316,183	137,361	130.1
Continental Oil (Del.)	2,643,820	2,200,527	20.2
Endicott-Johnson	1,223,236	438,665	178.9
Foster Wheeler Corp.	1,079,630	834,346	29.4
General Foods Co...	10,629,716	9,848,057	7.9
General Ry. Signal..	1,170,242	1,049,125	11.4
General Refractories.	1,381,516	1,206,310	14.6
Grand-Silver (F. & W.) Stores	792,408	699,028	13.4
Grand Union Co....	509,469	441,098	15.5
Houston Oil Co. (Texas)	1,014,417	779,422	30.4
Industrial Rayon Corp.	900,050	693,598	29.7
Int'l Business Machines	3,654,310	3,213,601	13.7
International Salt	*322,901	*231,298	39.6
International Shoe Co.	6,871,793	6,620,709	3.8
Kelvinator	2,298,025	1,715,053	34.0
Kimberly-Clark Corp.	1,827,400	1,666,259	9.7
McKeesport Tin Plate	1,513,830	1,084,562	28.4
Melville Shoe Corp..	955,705	727,069	31.5
National Dairy Products Corp.	12,947,211	7,638,943	69.5
Pacific Western Oil...	1,222,681	1,065,155	14.5
Paramount Publix ..	E8,434,000	5,130,000	64.3
Pub. Serv. Co. of No. Ill.	4,299,093	3,755,624	14.5
Radio-Keith-Orpheum	1,764,853	193,611	811.5
Scott Paper Co......	502,258	434,925	15.5
Superheater Corp....	2,435,677	2,209,810	10.2
Symington Co.	276,609	156,042	77.2
Telautograph Corp...	172,008	158,544	8.5
Transcontinental Oil.	*2,362,617	*1,715,822	37.8
United Biscuit Co. of Am.	996,296	839,153	18.7
United Fruit Co....	10,100,000	9,340,000	8.1
United Gas Improvement	19,962,973	16,348,298	22.1
United Rys. & Elec. Co. of Baltimore..	299,082	195,687	52.8
U. S. Pipe & Fdry. Co.	1,525,932	826,318	84.7
Warren Fdry. & Pipe	128,276	123,391	4.0
Wesson Oil & Snowdrift	*1,479,354	*706,298	109.4
White Rk. Miner. Sprig.	664,553	589,482	12.7
Whiskey (Wm.), Jr...	5,657,881	5,211,990	8.6
Yellow Truck & Coach Mfg.	1,437,863	859,659	67.2

*Before Federal taxes. *Combined second and third quarters ended May 31. E—Estimated.

Xcel Energy, and Exxon Mobil may continue to be around even if there's an unstable economy.

IS THIS STRATEGY FOR YOU?

With stocks, you have the excitement of the ups and downs of the market, so this is not a strategy for the conservative investor. A conservative investor might be happiest with little or no money in stocks, and even the most aggressive investor needs to have a high tolerance for risk to be able to stomach market volatility. Your time horizon should be long-term, seven or more years before you can begin assessing how your stocks are doing for you. The key to individual stock ownership is to invest into great companies with strong management teams forecasting growing business profits.

Factors such as sectors, styles, and sizes of companies can affect the risk and return of your stock choices. Look at the long-term track records of stocks that have consistent growth and a relatively low price relative to the company's earnings. You can do your research on Yahoo Finance, Google Finance, the Wall Street Journal online or Morningstar.com to name a few.

Stocks may be helpful to bypass roadblocks such as taxes, inflation, and running out of money when you get older. The potential growth of the stock market has proven to be substantially greater than bonds, cash, or inflation, according to Ibbotson's SBBI chart. If you are a growth or aggressive growth investor looking for the highest risk investments, consider a professionally managed portfolio of individual stocks.

The Money Game concept was used with permission from the book Stress-Free Retirement by Patrick Kelly.

S&P Composite Index
Log scale, annual

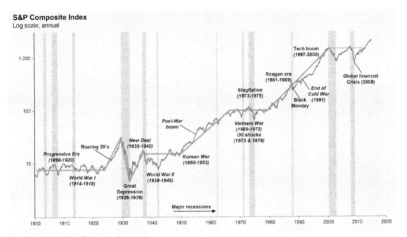

Source: Robert Shiller, FactSet, J.P. Morgan Asset Management
Data shown in log scale to best illustrate long-term index patterns
Past performance is not indicative of future returns. Chart is for illustrative purposes only
Data are as of March 31, 2015

CHAPTER II

INVESTMENT STRATEGY #2— EXCHANGE-TRADED FUNDS

THE COOL KIDS ON THE BLOCK

The second of three high-risk strategies in the Eight Investment Strategies for Life is exchange-traded funds or ETFs. A common definition of ETFs is "an investment vehicle combining key features of traditional mutual funds and individual stocks."

As we move the discussion from stocks to ETFs, you'll see that there are similarities and differences. Like index mutual funds, ETFs represent diversified portfolios of securities that track specific indexes. Like stocks, they can be bought and sold (long or short) in an exchange during a trading day, so if you want to sell your ETF at 10:15 a.m., you can.

In addition to trading flexibility, key ETF benefits include tax efficiency. ETFs are similar to stocks from a tax perspective— they are designed to be tax-deferred until they are sold. ETFs, like stocks, are taxed at a capital gains tax rate that is typically lower than tax on ordinary income.

ETFs differ from stocks in that they are generally diversified, with many stocks within one ETF. For example, you may want to purchase an ETF that represents the S&P 500 stock index. That ETF investment would emulate a basket of 500 stocks. This also means you can pick a style of stocks such as mid-cap stocks and purchase the ETF representing that style.

Another option is to choose a specific sector such as consumer discretionary stocks and purchase the ETF that has that representation. Let's say you want more exposure to East Asia, but you want a freer economy, such as Singapore. You can purchase an ETF representing a basket of stocks that make up the Singapore index.

Maybe you want some foreign currency exposure to Swiss francs or the Australian dollar; you can purchase that holding through an ETF. You may want to have alternative investments, such as coal, copper, frac sand, or gold; you can purchase an ETF to represent that sector in your portfolio.

ETFs can also behave like futures contracts or options. For example, you can purchase an ETF in an inverse fund that behaves in opposite correlation of the actual index, such as the S&P 500. Leveraged ETFs require the use of financial engineering techniques, including the use of equity swaps, derivatives and rebalancing, and re-indexing to achieve the desired return. The most common way to construct leveraged ETFs is by trading futures contracts.

ETFs have a management fee, but they may even be more tactical than stocks. Tactical ETFs mean having a manager who decides from time to time to move your money between asset classes, such as stocks, bonds, and cash. However, the majority of ETFs are built to simulate an index, which is not as actively managed. That's why most ETFs are lower cost.

ETFS VERSUS MUTUAL FUNDS

ETFs are investment vehicles designed to track market indexes that may represent hundreds or even thousands of securities.

They can offer ETF investors diversification of a typical index mutual fund with the trading flexibility of a stock. Anytime during the trading day, an investor can execute a single ETF trade and obtain broad exposure to an entire asset class, country, region, or sector. Mutual fund portfolios, on the other hand, are traded at the end of the trading day and cannot be traded during the day.

Learning the difference between ETFs and mutual funds may help you understand how tax efficient ETFs are. Since ETFs seek to track stock market indexes, their turnover is typically lower than that of actively managed mutual funds. Lower turnover can result in increased tax efficiency for investors when securities are sold at a gain. With traditional mutual funds, the buying and selling activities of some shareholders can trigger capital gains distributions for all of the fund's shareholders. For example, if the fund must sell a security to raise cash in order to meet redemptions, any related capital gains of that stock are distributed to all remaining investors in the fund.

In contrast, ETF trading occurs on an exchange just like a stock; there's no fund company in the middle. Thus, ETF investors are typically insulated from the tax consequences of fellow shareholders' actions and are primarily affected when they decide to sell the ETF, not when the money manager decides to sell a holding within the mutual fund.

In short, ETFs make it easier to see exactly what you own and what your fees are paying for. In this way, ETFs also offer transparencies of cost and holdings.

SHOULD YOU CONSIDER ETFS FOR YOUR PORTFOLIO?

ETFs provide a transparent, low-cost way to invest across asset classes and global markets for today's more dynamic, diverse portfolios.

Essentially, ETFs are a hybrid between a stock and a mutual fund. They're tax efficient, and they participate in the gains and losses of the market.

There are now more ETFs than mutual funds, and you can isolate the types of sectors and styles of investments or even geographic regions that you're investing in through an ETF. For example, the S&P 500 is an index that is mirrored by an ETF. So you can buy an S&P 500 ETF, or you could buy an ETF that holds real estate, gold, commodities, or stocks of one particular economy or country such as Canada or Australia. You can buy an ETF that only invests in hardwood lumber, one that only invests in copper, or one that's tied just to the automotive industry.

More information about ETFs can be found on services such as Morningstar.

An ETF can be considered a high-risk strategy if the index that it's buying into is a more volatile index. For example, bioscience or pharmaceutical companies may be more volatile than a megacap index composed of the largest companies in the world. A smaller-company ETF may be much more risky than a larger-company ETF or a bond ETF that specializes in short-term investment grade bonds.

Still, ETFs are popular, because they are lower cost and are a transparent approach to investing. When you purchase an ETF you know exactly what you're getting, and you're getting it at a lower cost. Plus, you can purchase a diversified portfolio of ETFs and own a representation of hundreds of thousands of different stocks instead of just a few.

An ETF may dramatically reduce the business risk that's present when you purchase an individual stock. So if you bought an S&P 500 index and it happened to have Enron on that index, it would be one out of 500 stocks that would go broke, which wouldn't affect your portfolio very much at all. ETFs eliminate that business risk but still let you own a slice of that particular sector of the stock market performance.

ROADBLOCKS AVOIDED

ETFs may help you bypass the stock market losses roadblock if you choose more conservative dividend-paying stock or bond ETFs, commodities ETFs, or noncorrelated ETFs.

ETFs are also very tax efficient; the tax ramifications of an ETF are very similar to those of a stock. You typically don't pay tax on an ETF until it's sold. However, you do pay tax on the dividends that are issued by the underlying stocks.

The running out of money roadblock might be avoided if you earn dividends through dividend-paying stocks, interest-bearing bonds, or interest-bearing bond ETFs.

Using ETFs to possibly avoid the unstable economy roadblock means investing in stock market investments that are not correlated to the market. You can also invest outside of the country that's having an unstable economy. For example, when most of the currencies of the world were having trouble back in 2010, the Swiss franc was rocketing to record highs. Other currencies that were doing better were currencies in asset-rich countries such as Norway, Australia, and Canada.

ETFs may be a big inflation hedge if you purchase an index of either equity investments or real estate. The road block of inflation may be overcome through owning various ETFs that own stocks of large, medium or small companies of US or international companies. Real Estate Investment Trusts or REITS may also be publically traded in an ETF format. Real estate, stocks and even commodities may have an inflation hedging component that you may want to consider using within your own portfolio.

CHAPTER 11 TAKEAWAYS:

THE FOLLOWING IS A SHORT LIST OF A
FEW DOZEN CATEGORIES OF ETFS:

Stock ETFs
Broad Market ETFs
Large Cap Stock ETFs
Mid Cap Stock ETFs
Small Cap Stock ETFs
Factor ETFs
Dividend and Income ETFs
Consumer ETFs
Energy ETFs
Financial ETFs
Health Care ETFs
Industrial ETFs
Material ETFs
Telecommunications ETFs
Technology ETFs
Utilities ETFs
Real Estate ETFs
Asset Allocation ETFs
Minimum Volatility ETFs
Factor ETFs
Social/Environmental ETFs
Commodities ETFs
Futures/Equity-Based ETFs
Producer Equity ETFs
Physical Asset Based ETFs (Gold and Silver)
Futures Based Products ETFs
World Markets ETFs
Developed Markets ETFs
Emerging Markets ETFs
Single Country ETFs

Bond ETFs
US Government Bond ETFs
Inflation Bond ETFs
International Government Bond ETFs
Corporate Bond ETFs
International Bond ETFs
Emerging Market Bond ETFs

CHAPTER 12

INVESTMENT STRATEGY #3—MUTUAL FUNDS

HOW MUCH DO YOU REALLY KNOW?

A mutual fund is really an investment company. When you own a share of a mutual fund, you don't actually own the underlying stocks or bonds directly; instead, you own shares of an investment company.

The first invest-
ment company was
formed on March
21, 1924 as Mas-
sachusetts Investors
Trust, by Massa-
chusetts Financial
Services, or MFS. In
its infancy, America's

oldest mutual fund, Massachusetts Investors Trust or MIT, held bank, insurance, industrial, railroad, and public utilities stocks of companies such as US Steel, General Motors, Union Pacific Railroad, General Electric, and AT&T. MIT is still operating in

2015 with over $7.51 billion in asset under management (MFS. com, 07/31/15).

Mutual funds are invested in a basket of stocks or bonds or alternative investments. Usually, a money manager or a team of portfolio managers runs the money for the mutual fund.

The mutual funds usually are invested in a particular style or sector of the stock market. Styles of stocks include large-, medium-, and small-company growth, blended, and value stocks. Sectors include consumer staples, consumer discretionary, industrial, energy, health care, real estate, pharmaceuticals, biotechnology, technology, utilities, manufacturing, transportation, and telecomunications in both US and international stocks.

The mutual fund manager's objective is to squeeze out the highest risk-adjusted return for the shareholders. Because the mutual fund industry is so competitive, the money manager or portfolio management team is always looking for ways to add better performance to their portfolio without taking extraordinary risk. Consumers really decide what funds they want to invest in, and they gravitate toward quality funds with solid performance histories, consistent management teams, and low fees. The funds can receive higher scores oftentimes based on high risk-adjusted returns. Fiduciary responsibility and organizational ratings are becoming more important in holding fund managers to higher ethical standards.

TRACKING PERFORMANCE

You can track the performance of your investments through Google Finance, Yahoo Finance, or Morningstar, to name a few.

Usually these services list past performance, investment manager fees, and manager tenure, and give a rating of one to five stars for an investment's risk-adjusted return.

Those mutual funds with the highest risk-adjusted return over three years typically get a five-star rating from Morningstar, the best you can get. There are other ways to analyze mutual funds, such as style, drift, and corporate culture.

Some mutual funds tend to drift away from their original intent. For example, a large-company stock fund may purchase small-cap stocks in order to boost its performance, thereby drifting away from its original intent of being a large-company stock fund.

Care must be taken in understanding the style that's appropriate for your risk tolerance.

An example of style is a stock fund manager that's focused on large-company value stocks and usually invests in banks and utility companies or manufacturing stocks that are more conservative. Often, however, the growth stocks are in the higher-priced stocks such as technology stocks; some value stock managers will purchase technology stocks from time to time to boost performance. They also may be taking on more risk, and investors may not realize that they have a riskier fund than they thought they had.

The mutual fund style is explained in its prospectus. Within the prospectus are the objectives of the fund and all the operations and costs that go into running a mutual fund. The management team is listed in the prospectus, as well as the other details pertinent to managing the investment company.

CHOOSING A MUTUAL FUND

An example of a mutual fund approach comes from Dave Ramsey in his book *Total Money Makeover.* He suggests drawing a circle on a sheet of paper and putting an "X" through it, dividing your circle into four equal slices: 25 percent each of international stocks, large-company stocks, medium-size company stocks, and small-company stocks.

Ramsey suggests considering one mutual fund to fit in each of those four slices—a fund that has the highest risk-adjusted return, the lowest cost, and the longest manager-tenure possible. Search for these managers through a service like Morningstar, or you may want to hire a retirement wealth advisor to help do the analysis for you.

Mutual funds may be a higher-risk strategy if your fund is invested completely into stocks. Mutual funds, however, can also be invested in bonds of short-, intermediate-, or long-term maturities. Bond categories may include corporate, government, or international bonds.

Mutual funds invested in bonds are open-ended and might have a higher interest-rate risk, because you are not guaranteed to get your principal value back upon selling your shares. If interest rates go up, bond values typically go down. Like a teeter-totter, there is an inverse relationship between interest rates and bond values.

The simplest approach to putting together a mutual fund portfolio is to set up criteria for decision making. For example, if you wanted to use higher risk-adjusted returns in your portfolio, you could look for five-star mutual funds that are invested in securities appropriate to your risk tolerance and that have excellent one, three, five, and ten-year histories. Ideally, these mutual funds would have long manager tenure and a lower expense ratio.

ADDITIONAL COSTS

Beware of trading costs. What you may perceive as a low-cost mutual fund may actually cost three to five times more than you thought. Research the internal trading costs of your mutual funds today and add it to your annual expense ratio found in your prospectus to discover your true annual expense ratio. Contact your retirement wealth advisor to help you calculate your total hidden mutual fund costs.

Taxes affect your investments whether you sell them or not in a mutual fund. Even if you held your shares through bear markets, the money manager may sell some of the holdings, triggering a realized capital gain. So even though your fund may be losing money, you still may have to pay substantial taxes on your mutual fund.

Therefore, we like to use mutual funds within IRAs and other tax-deferred qualified plans, such as a 401(k) plan. Holding individual stocks and ETFs outside of your IRAs and tax-qualified plans may help keep your taxes as low as possible.

Roadblocks Avoided

Using mutual funds in your portfolio may help bypass the stock market losses roadblock if you use a noncorrelated investment such as a bond mutual fund. You can also avoid the taxes roadblock by purchasing a mutual fund with a low turnover ratio in a more passive investment style.

Mutual funds may help you keep pace with inflation and the risk of running out of money down the road. However, mutual funds can also cause your principal value to go down if invested in stocks when the overall market drops. All investments have risk including loss of principal; past performance is no guarantee on future results. Mutual funds may help you diversify enough to potentially overcome the roadblock of an unstable economy.

If you would like to proceed to the design of a proper mutual fund plan, contact your retirement wealth advisor.

CHAPTER 12 TAKEAWAYS:

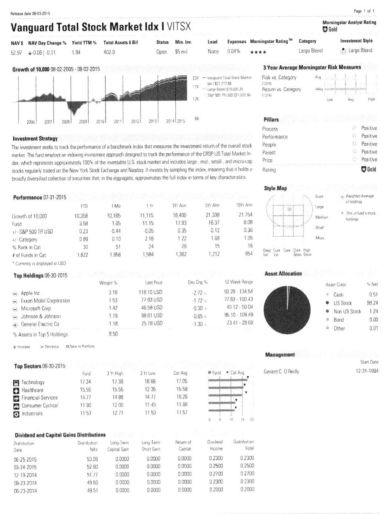

Vanguard Total Stock Market Idx I VITSX

Morningstar Analyst Rating
Gold

NAV $	NAV Day Change %	Yield TTM %	Total Assets $ Bil	Status	Min. Inv.	Load	Expenses	Morningstar Rating™	Category	Investment Style
52.97	-0.06	-0.11	1.84	402.9	Open	$5 mil	None	0.04%	★★★★	Large Blend	Large Blend

Growth of 10,000 08-02-2005 - 08-02-2015

22K — Vanguard Total Stock Market Idx / $21,717.59
17K --- Large Blend $19,605.25
12K --- S&P 500 TR USD $21,022.84
6K

2006 2007 2008 2009 2010 2011 2012 2013 2014 2015

3 Year Average Morningstar Risk Measures

Risk vs. Category	Avg	
(1374)		
Return vs. Category	+Avg	
(1374)		

Low Avg High

Investment Strategy

The investment seeks to track the performance of a benchmark index that measures the investment return of the overall stock market. The fund employs an indexing investment approach designed to track the performance of the CRSP US Total Market Index, which represents approximately 100% of the investable U.S. stock market and includes large-, mid-, small-, and micro-cap stocks regularly traded on the New York Stock Exchange and Nasdaq. It invests by sampling the index, meaning that it holds a broadly diversified collection of securities that, in the aggregate, approximates the full index in terms of key characteristics.

Pillars

Process	⊕	Positive
Performance	⊕	Positive
People	⊕	Positive
Parent	⊕	Positive
Price	⊕	Positive
Rating		Gold

Performance 07-31-2015

	YTD	1 Mo	1 Yr	3Yr Ann	5Yr Ann	10Yr Ann
Growth of 10,000	10,358	10,165	11,115	16,400	21,338	21,754
Fund	3.58	1.65	11.15	17.93	16.37	8.08
+/- S&P 500 TR USD	0.23	-0.44	-0.05	0.35	0.12	0.36
+/- Category	0.89	0.10	2.18	1.22	1.68	1.05
% Rank in Cat	30	51	24	28	15	16
# of Funds in Cat	1,622	1,656	1,584	1,382	1,212	854

* Currency is displayed in USD

Style Map

Giant — ⊕ Weighted Average of holdings
Large — ● 75% of fund's stock holdings
Medium
Small
Micro

Deep Core Core Core High
Val Val Grow Grow

Top Holdings 06-30-2015

	Weight %	Last Price	Day Chg %	52 Week Range
⊝ Apple Inc	3.18	118.10 USD	-2.72 ↓	93.28 - 134.54
⊝ Exxon Mobil Corporation	1.53	77.93 USD	-1.72 ↓	77.63 - 100.43
⊝ Microsoft Corp	1.42	46.59 USD	-0.30 ↓	40.12 - 50.04
⊝ Johnson & Johnson	1.19	99.61 USD	-0.85 ↓	95.10 - 109.49
⊕ General Electric Co	1.18	25.78 USD	-1.30 ↓	23.41 - 28.68
% Assets in Top 5 Holdings	8.50			

⊕ Increase   ⊝ Decrease   ⊙ New to Portfolio

Asset Allocation

	Asset Class	% Net
⊙	Cash	0.51
●	US Stock	98.24
●	Non US Stock	1.24
⊙	Bond	0.00
⊙	Other	0.01

Top Sectors 06-30-2015

	Fund	3 Yr High	3 Yr Low	Cat Avg
Technology	17.34	17.38	18.66	17.05
Healthcare	15.55	15.55	12.35	15.59
Financial Services	14.77	14.88	14.77	16.26
Consumer Cyclical	11.90	12.00	11.43	11.88
Industrials	11.53	12.71	11.53	11.57

■ Fund   ▼ Cat Avg

0   5   10   15   20

Management

	Start Date
Gerard C. O'Reilly	12-31-1994

Dividend and Capital Gains Distributions

Distribution Date	Distribution NAV	Long-Term Capital Gain	Long-Term Short Gain	Return of Capital	Dividend Income	Distribution Total
06-25-2015	53.09	0.0000	0.0000	0.0000	0.2300	0.2300
03-24-2015	52.80	0.0000	0.0000	0.0000	0.2500	0.2500
12-19-2014	51.77	0.0000	0.0000	0.0000	0.2700	0.2700
09-23-2014	49.60	0.0000	0.0000	0.0000	0.2300	0.2300
06-23-2014	49.51	0.0000	0.0000	0.0000	0.2000	0.2000

MORNINGSTAR®

Helping our clients retire with confidence since 1984

Basic Scatter Plot

Prepared on: 7/28/2015 | Fund data as of 6/30/2015

Prepared By:

Brent Welch
Welshire Capital, LLC
9538 East 16 Frontage Road
Onalaska, WI 54650

Welshire Capital, LLC· 9538 E 16 Frontage Rd, · Onalaska, WI 54650 (608) 783-0003 · 1-800-TAX PLAN · Fax (608) 782-0002 Securities offered through Comprehensive Asset Management and Servicing, Inc. (CAMAS), 1-800-637-3211, member FINRA/SIPC/MSRB, Brent Welch Registered Representative. Advisory services offered through Welshire Capital, LLC, a Registered Investment Adviser located in Wisconsin. Welshire Capital, LLC and CAMAS are separate and unrelated companies. www.WelshireCapital.com

fi360°

Fi360 Fiduciary Score® Breakdown (Funds/ETFs/GRPAs only)

fi360 Fiduciary Score Criteria

1. Inception Date: The investment must have at least a 3 year track history.
2. Manager Tenure: The investment manager must have at least a 2 year track history. (Most senior manager's tenure)
3. Assets: The investment must have at least 75 million under management. (Total across all share classes for funds/etfs)
4. Composition: The investment's allocation to its primary asset class should be greater than or equal to 80%. (Not applied to all peer groups)
5. Style: The investment's current style box should match the peer group. (Not applied to all peer groups)
6. Prospectus Net Exp Ratio: The investment must place in the top 75% of its peer group.
7. Alpha: The investment must place in the top 50% of its peer group.
8. Sharpe: The investment must place in the top 50% of its peer group.
9. 1 Year Return: The investment must place in the top 50% of its peer group.
10. 3 Year Return: The investment must place in the top 50% of its peer group.
11. 5 Year Return: The investment must place in the top 50% of its peer group.

Calculation Methodology

The fi360 Fiduciary Score is a peer percentile ranking of an investment against a set of quantitative due diligence criteria selected to reflect prudent fiduciary management. The criteria include total returns, risk-adjusted returns, expenses, and other portfolio statistics. Investments are ranked according to their ability to meet due diligence criteria every month. The rank becomes the fi360 Fiduciary Score. The fi360 Fiduciary Score Average is a one-, three-, five- or ten-year rolling average of an investments fi360 Fiduciary Score. The fi360 Fiduciary Score represents a suggested course of action and is not intended, nor should it be used, as the sole source of information for reaching an investment decision. Visit the Glossary or fi360.com/fi360-Fiduciary-Score for more information.

Legend

√ Investment meets the criterion

X Investment does not meet the criterion

N/Av Investment data is not available

N/S Investment doesn't have the history to be scored

N/App Investment is not screened on the criterion

Investment Name	Peer Group	fi360 Fiduciary Score Average					fi360 Fiduciary Score Criteria										
		Score	1 Yr	3 Yr	5 Yr	10 Yr	1	2	3	4	5	6	7	8	9	10	11
Large-Cap Equity																	
Vanguard Total Stock Market Idx I (VITSX)	Large Blend						√	√	√	√	√	√	√	√	√	√	√
	# of Peers 1,380	1,275	1,118	1,018	567												

fi360_Portrait_v6_0

fi360°

Fund data as of 6/30/2015

Fi360 Fiduciary Score® Scatter Plot

The fi360 Fiduciary Score is a peer percentile ranking of an investment against a set of quantitative due diligence criteria selected to reflect prudent fiduciary management. The criteria include total returns, risk-adjusted returns, expenses, and other portfolio statistics. Investments are ranked according to their ability to meet due diligence criteria every month. The rank becomes the fi360 Fiduciary Score. The fi360 Fiduciary Score Average is a one-, three-, five- or ten-year rolling average of an investments fi360 Fiduciary Score. The fi360 Fiduciary Score represents a suggested course of action and is not intended, nor should it be used, as the sole source of information for reaching an investment decision. Visit the Glossary or fi360.com/fi360-Fiduciary-Score for more information.

				fi360 Fiduciary Score				
					Average			
ID	Investment Name (Ticker)	Type		Score	1 Yr	3 Yr	5 Yr	10 Yr
Investments Shown in the Scatter Plot								
1	Vanguard Total Stock Market Idx I (VITSX)	MF						
			# of Peers	1,380	1,275	1,118	1,018	567

fi360®

Fi360 Fiduciary Score® Scatter Plot (Cont.)

fi360 Fiduciary Score Scatter Plot

The chart plots each scored investment using the fi360 Fiduciary Score Average (3-Year) on the vertical axis and the fi360 Fiduciary Score on the horizontal axis. Green, yellow and red lines are drawn to highlight the different fi360 Fiduciary Score quartiles. Investments in the bottom left corner of the chart have a better Score.

Bubble sizes are based on the $ amount invested. | Bubble numbers refer to the Investment ID's on the previous page.

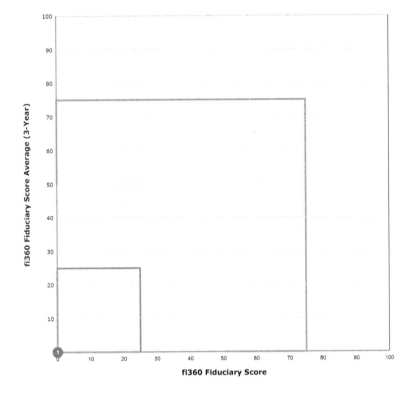

fi360_Portrait_v6_0

Fund data as of 6/30/2015

Disclosure

All data has been obtained from third parties and is deemed to be accurate. Welshire Capital, LLC has not made attempts to audit the accuracy of the included information provided by third parties.

fi360_Portrait_v6_0

fi360°

Fund data as of 6/30/2015

DO YOU KNOW?

You can still be taxed even if you don't sell the mutual fund?

You don't actually own the stocks; you own a share of an investment company?

Whether the stocks in your mutual fund will do well in a tough economy?

What's the cost of your mutual fund?

How long has your mutual fund manager been managing your mutual fund?

How long has the investment company been managing the mutual fund?

CHAPTER 13

INVESTMENT STRATEGY #4— INVESTMENT AIRBAGS

CAN THEY SAVE YOUR FINANCIAL LIFE?

Stocks, ETFs, and mutual funds are types of high-risk strategies suitable for a more aggressive investor or a younger investor. If you are approaching retirement or are already retired, you may want to consider some moderate strategies for your investment portfolio.

GUARANTEED INCOME FOR LIFE

My son just got broadsided by a large SUV. The collision was shocking enough to deploy his side air bags in his new used car. His head jolted hard to his left as the air bag popped open between his head and the window. I believe that the air bag saved him from a more serious injury. Just as air bags in your car can help you stay healthy in the event of a big crash, investment air bags may help save you financially when the next big stock market crash happens.

When you bought your last car, did you think about the cost of the air bags as part of the expense? Did the major criteria for choosing the car you purchased include the cost of maintaining the air bags? Did you even ask your car dealership what the cost of the air bags was as a percentage of your car price or even as just a straight number?

We don't really consider the air bags in our car as a deterrent when purchasing our car. In fact, to the contrary, we don't really want to buy a car without air bags.

If you think about it, in the event of a big crash, air bags could save your life. Why wouldn't you want air bags? In fact, why wouldn't you want five or six air bags in your car? In addition to the one that pops out of the steering wheel, why not have air bags that protect you and your passenger on all sides?

Imagine being able to have investment air bags installed on part of your investment portfolio. Yes, there's a higher cost for this moderate-risk strategy, but in the event of a big market crash, they may save your financial life.

HOW INVESTMENT AIRBAGS WORK

Investment air bags are set up to create a second set of numbers. These numbers are usually called your guaranteed income base, from which guaranteed income is derived. Adversaries call this second set of numbers "funny money," but in my opinion there's nothing really funny about guaranteed income for life. In fact, why not call this your "serious money"?

When you use the word "guarantee" with your investments, you're most frequently talking about an insurance company of some type. Aren't they the ones that insured your parents' and grandparents' pensions? Aren't they the ones that insured pension plans in the state that you live in or in large companies that you may know about? Insurance companies can provide guaranteed income you can't outlive.

So the insurance company sets up a separate set of books for your investments. Variable annuities are one of the platforms upon which the guaranteed income rider is placed. The guaranteed income base is established, and it can grow at a percentage of 5 to 7 percent per year or the highest stock market growth. Imagine an income base that could only grow year after year until you're in your 80s or 90s. It cannot go down in value; it's an income base that's there for you in the event that the stock market drops dramatically.

You can use top name-brand mutual fund managers to run your money within your variable annuities (VAs). Vanguard, Black Rock, T. Rowe Price, Fidelity, J.P. Morgan, and American Funds are a few of the money managers that come to my mind who run money in various VAs. The mutual-fund-like accounts within a VA are called separate accounts. Separate accounts may invest in large company stocks, international stocks, or even mid- or small-cap company stocks. You could invest in alternative investments or biotech companies or sectors such as technology or utilities if you wanted to. There are also bond options and guaranteed options within the variable annuity chassis. Your investments are built on that chassis according to your customized risk tolerance. The cost of your VA separate accounts are around 1 percent and then you add management and expense fees of about 1.6 percent. The total costs are around 2.6 percent for your VA chassis.

Then you can choose an optional guaranteed income rider, also known as investment air bags. This guaranteed income rider will grow at a specific percentage and lock in any stock market gains. The cost for your income rider may be approximately 1.4

percent. When added to the VA chassis costs subtotaling 2.6 percent, you might be paying around 4 percent per year for a VA with investment airbags. Keep in mind that the upside limit of your VA is uncapped, meaning that if your S&P 500 index separate account is up 10 percent for the year, you may earn that 10 percent (minus the VA costs of 4 percent) leaving you with a net gain of 6 percent. This calculation is not meant to be indicative to all VAs. Past performance is no guarantee of future success. All expenses for VAs vary, and the prospectus must be read in order to understand all risks, expenses, benefits and potential rewards.

When you decide to flip the switch for guaranteed lifetime income for you and/or your spouse if you're married, you can derive that guaranteed income for life from your guaranteed income base.

That base might be designed to go up with the stock market. It generally goes down if you pull all your money out or if there's no money left in your contract—then of course the contract with its benefits will lapse.

Investment air bags offer the upside potential of the market with potentially less downside risk. Your guaranteed income base loses zero when the market goes down, but if the market goes up 10 percent, you might make 6 percent.

However, different than the safe strategies, which will be discussed in the following chapters, your actual account value can drop.

That's where the risk is taken on by the consumer. If your portfolio is invested 100 percent in stocks and the stock market drops 50 percent, the value of your account could drop 50 percent. Even with a 50 percent drop in the market you still may qualify for guaranteed income for that didn't drop 50 percent. In the event that your stocks went south, you still may have the ability to get income for the rest of your life from the guaranteed income base.

AIRBAG FEES

Investment air bags may help grow your money at the speed of the stock market minus the fees that they charge for the air bags. And those fees can be expensive.

As previously expressed, one of the biggest disadvantages of VAs with investment airbags are the high fees. With the separate account fees at approximately 1 percent, the management and expense fees at about 1.6 percent and the investment airbags cost of 1.4 percent or so, you may be paying 4 percent or more in fees.

However, the investment air bag number, otherwise known as the guaranteed income base, grows at a speed that's not reduced by those investment charges. Those fees do erode your actual account balance. Ask your registered representative if the VA income rider costs are calculated in the guaranteed income base value or the account value.

Let's say the stock market performs as well as it has in the past even though there's no guarantee it will continue to do so. Even with the 4 percent charge, you just might have some type of a growth on your underlying investments and be protected with the source of guaranteed income.

Variable annuities also have a surrender charge that may last four to seven years. During this time, many companies offer you a 10 percent free withdrawal that makes the surrender charge less of a concern. However, make sure that you have sufficient liquidity outside of the variable annuity for income and emergency expenses.

We don't recommend a VA for all of your money in your portfolio. However, it may be appropriate for some of your money, especially for the moderate portion of your overall investment allocation.

Some higher-risk investors may also find investment air bags appealing, or they may be more comfortable with a higher-risk investment such as stocks, ETFs, or mutual funds.

ROADBLOCKS AVOIDED

Investment air bags may help bypass the stock market losses and taxes roadblocks because the investment air bags are built on a tax-deferred variable annuity chassis.

They may also benefit in the old-age illness roadblock, since a variable annuity chassis typically has a surrender charge that can last up to seven years or more. For example, the chart below shows a seven-year surrender charge starting at 7 percent and declining to 1 percent. Typically during those seven years, you can receive 10 percent as a free withdrawal. Most people don't find that to be an obstacle, because they're not pulling all their money out at retirement, they're only pulling income off their investments. Income today is usually less than 5 percent per year.

YEAR	1	2	3	4	5	6	7
CDSC[1]	7%	6%	5%	4%	3%	2%	1%
FREE $[2]	10%	10%	10%	10%	10%	10%	10%

1 CDSC: Contingent Deferred Sales Charge

2 Free $: The free withdrawl rate that you can take without triggering the CDSC (this is a sample, please review prospectus for details on the variable annuity you are considering).

Old-age illnesses, such as not being able to perform two out of six activities of daily living, could allow you to take out withdrawals with no surrender charges. Also, if you develop some type of life-threatening illness, the surrender charges may be waived.

Investment air bags may also keep you from running out of money. They are a great way to keep your money invested in separate accounts operated like a mutual fund and still have a guarantee in the event of a dramatic drop in the stock market or a period of flat performance.

The unstable economy roadblocks could also be bypassed because of the variable annuities with guaranteed income riders, otherwise known as investment air bags. If the stock market plummets during an upcoming economic earthquake, your VA with a guaranteed income may help you receive guaranteed income for life for you and if you are married, for your spouse. Wouldn't it be nice to have more guaranteed income like your Social Security even during the hardest of times?

The inflation roadblock can also be bypassed, because you can choose those investments that are historically recognized to hedge against inflation, such as stocks and real estate.

As for the no plan roadblock, one could argue that even if you didn't have a plan, investment air bags could still give you guaranteed income for life, which may help you achieve some of your other goals.

CHAPTER 13 TAKEAWAYS:

THE INVESTMENT RISK PYRAMID

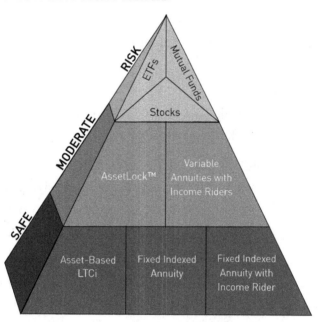

RISK LEVEL

← ————— LOW | HIGH ————— →

	Asset Based LTC i	Fixed Indexed Annuity[1]	Fixed Indexed Annuity[2] with Income Rider	Asset-Lock™ with Formula Folios	Variable Annuity with Income Rider	Stocks	Mutual Funds	Index ETFs
Welshire 100 (E)	5%	0%	0%	20%	15%	20%	20%	20%
Welshire 80 (D)	5%	0%	15%	20%	20%	15%	15%	10%
Welshire 60 (C)	5%	15%	20%	30%	30%	0%	0%	0%
Welshire 40 (B)	5%	25%	30%	20%	20%	0%	0%	0%
Welshire 20 (A)	5%	40%	35%	10%	10%	0%	0%	0%

INVESTMENT STRATEGY #5— ASSETLOCK OR THE WELSHIRE^{SM} ADVANCE AND PROTECT STRATEGY

WILL IT WORK FOR YOU?

Moderate investing may include computerized sell strategies, such as AssetLock, or a tactical investment strategy, such as Welshire^{SM} Advance and Protect.

ASSETLOCK

You are in charge of your retirement, and you deserve to know about AssetLock technology.

For selling out of your portfolio, AssetLock creates a target at a certain percentage below your high watermark (a high watermark is the value of your portfolio tracked every day to determine the highest level your portfolio has ever achieved). AssetLock technology monitors your investments every day, 24/7, and lets you know when your portfolio hits a new record high. When it does, the AssetLock technology raises your targeted sell strategy to that level.

For example, if you chose a 5 percent AssetLock and your portfolio rose 10 percent, your AssetLock would increase 10 percent as well, so that your new targeted sell strategy would be 5 percent above your original investment.

Leonardo da Vinci said simplicity is the ultimate sophistication. AssetLock is designed to help you protect your gains so you can help protect your future. Each day, AssetLock tracks your portfolio relative to your all-time high watermark.

Based on your unique profile, you'll also be tracking your AssetLock Value. This value becomes the exit button for your portfolio, allowing you to invest with confidence and always know the limit your portfolio might decline before fully removed from the markets.

Since the AssetLock value is updated each time your portfolio reaches an all-time high, you're also creating a new and higher AssetLock Value.

AssetLock is a revolutionary way to monitor your portfolio and invest with confidence. We believe this combination is a smart, secure, and simple approach.

AssetLock is a technology that helps you reduce your downside risk for your investment portfolio. You may set the downside target to 5 percent or 7.5, 15, or 20 percent below the high water mark of your investment portfolio. When your portfolio hits new record highs, you will be notified by a text or email to your smart phone, tablet or computer. Each time your portfolio hits a new high water mark, your AssetLock level raises accordingly. A great day for any investor with AssetLock is the day their AssetLock value reaches their original investment amount. Some call it "playing with the house's money" when your AssetLock value is at or above your original investment level. That means you have targeted your AssetLock technology to sell your positions when your account triggers the AssetLock level.

AssetLock technology is popular because you can add another layer of safety to your investment portfolio that may have mutual funds, ETFs, or individual stocks. AssetLock targets a level to sell off your more risky investments in exchange for more conservative ones. For example, if you chose a 15 percent AssetLock level, when your portfolio drops from its high water mark to 15 percent less breaking through AssetLock, the technology makes the sell orders. Please keep in mind that stocks and ETFs can trade "at the market" during the day but mutual funds must trade at end of the day pricing. There is no guarantee that the 15 percent AssetLock level is an absolute, however, it is a targeted value that triggers the sell orders that trade as soon as administratively possible. The values may drop below the AssetLock value. Even so, there may be peace of mind knowing that your AssetLock value is targeted to a certain percentage below your high water mark of either 5 percent or 7.5 percent or 15 percent or 20 percent. Isn't it good to know that you have a sell system in place if the stock market plummets once again?

WELSHIRE^{SM} ADVANCE AND PROTECT

The Welshire^{SM} Advance and Protect strategy is designed to help you keep your money in the right place at the right time. The Welshire^{SM} Investment Policy Committee (IPC) may actually do something to change your portfolio in the face of danger. For example, if you're sailing across a lake and you see a storm coming and you're unable to get to shore, you'd want to drop the mainsail and probably power up your engine to hold your position as the storm blows over. If you kept your mainsail up, you'd get blown off course dramatically and put yourself in harm's way.

With tactical investing such as the Welshire^{SM} Advance and Protect strategy, your money managers can "drop your main sail" by reducing your stock exposure when fundamental or technical indicators forecast a much weaker economy.

Giving the investment manager the ability to make changes for you can give you peace of mind knowing that they're doing something with your money.

THE RIGHT STRATEGY

Do you remember back in 2008 or 2009 when your broker might have told you to just hang in there? Your current investment advisor might have told you to buy, hold, and hope. But is hope really a strategy?

Just think back to the action America took in the aftermath of the events of September 11, 2001, when terrorists attacked our country on our soil; the president's plan was to declare war on terrorism, a counterattack. I remember how difficult it was to do investment reviews with clients after 9/11. Our financial system was reeling from the aftershock of the terrorist attacks. Clients were worried, and they wanted to know what to do with their money. One day, I drove home to have lunch and had to lie down for a five-minute nap. During that nap, I thought to myself, "Just like President Bush declared war on terrorism, I need to declare war on stock market terrorism." That's when our firm developed the Welshire^{SM} Advance and Protect Strategy—back in 2001.

Part of protecting what's yours is doing something when it needs to be done—creating a war on stock market terrorism, essentially. Not basing your investment strategy on feelings but on formula; not basing it on emotions but on a process.

Welshire^{SM} may implore various investment firms that have proven track records and put them together in a portfolio and can help create a tactical strategy that may work for you. Multiple money managers are superior to one manager, since each formulaic process may perform differently during various market cycles. For example, during a saw tooth market, when the stock index goes up and down so quickly the pattern develops like a saw blade, a more passive formulaic approach may be better. During a cyclical bear market, a more sensitive, quick-responding process may save more money for you.

100 PERCENT LIQUIDITY

The Welshire^{SM} Advance and Protect Strategy is a 100 percent liquid, fee-only wealth management strategy. As a fee-only investment model, you can put your money in one day and take it out the next and not be charged a penalty or commission. However, your custodian will probably charge you a fee if you decide to close your IRA account. There are no commissions paid to your Welshire^{SM} Retirement Wealth Advisor for the Welshire^{SM} Advance & Protect strategy.

You may decide to hold your investment for a very long time. The good news is that you only pay the fee while you have money in your account, and you will probably only pay for the management of your portfolio when you can justify the value is there for you. That value might not be in making you rich but rather in helping you from becoming poor.

The Welshire^{SM} Advance and Protect strategy is not as tax efficient as other strategies, such as ETFs or individual stocks, because the money manager can make tactical decisions such as reducing your stock exposure when an economic storm appears imminent. This could trigger taxes whether you like it or not.

The taxation on Welshire^{SM} Advance & Protect may even be higher than a mutual fund because the manager will sell certain holdings, which may trigger taxes in your portfolio. The Welshire^{SM} Advance & Protect works well with IRA money and qualified plan money rolled over from a 401(k) or 403(b), profit-sharing plans, or pension plans. Since Welshire^{SM} Advance & Protect is a tactical model with frequent buys and sells possible, holding it within a tax-deferred retirement account makes a lot of sense.

Welshire's^{SM} Advance and Protect strategy uses a concept called portfolio rotation to take risk off or put risk back into a portfolio. Welshire^{SM} uses five models from conservative to aggressive, models A through E. The A model uses a target of 20% in stocks, B targets 40% stocks, C 60%, D 80% and E 100% stocks. The A model is also known as the Welshire^{SM} 20 because of it's targeted 20% stock exposure.

Portfolio rotation works like this; suppose an economic storm was seen brewing on the horizon and the Investment Committee decided to move to protect the models. Then, if you were in the Welshire^{SM} 60, or C model, you would have had a targeted 60% stock exposure. The committee may have moved you down one notch to 40% stocks. This move would have taken approximately 20% of the stocks off the table.

If the storm was severe, the committee may rotate you two notches down from 60% to 20% in stock exposure. When the committee sees that the coast is clear, they can begin rotating your model back up from A to B and then from B to C. This gives you a picture of how portfolio rotation works with the Welshire^{SM} Advance and Protect strategy.

ROADBLOCKS AVOIDED

AssetLock technology may help you avoid the roadblocks of stock market losses, running out of money, and an unstable economy (due to terrorism, a medical pandemic, or other potentially economic catastrophe) because it limits your downside risk. For example, if you had all your money in an S&P 500 fund that lost 50 percent, you'd lose 50 percent of your money. If your AssetLock was set at 5 percent, your targeted downside risk would be at 5 percent. Because the sell orders are triggered during the day at that 5 percent level, your portfolio may lose more than 5 percent (or whatever your AssetLock level is set at).

Welshire^{SM} Advance & Protect may help beat inflation, because it can hold stocks or real estate in your overall asset allocation. There are five risk-based models from moderate to aggressive growth. They range from conservative through aggressive. The Advance & Protect (A&P) A model is the conservative and the A&P E model is aggressive.

AssetLock technology may help bypass the roadblock of not having a plan because it automatically tracks your portfolio 24/7, 365 days a year, and adjusts the downside loss limit every time your portfolio hits a new market high or a high watermark. This is a plan that may help you keep together what you worked so hard to put together.

Disclaimer: AssetLock and Welshire^{SM} are separate and unrelated companies. Past performance is no guarantee of future results. All investments have risk including the loss of principle.

Chapters 10, 11, and 12 discussed the higher-risk strategies of stocks, ETFs, and mutual funds. This chapter concludes the discussion of moderate-risk strategies including investment air bags, AssetLock technology, and the Welshire^{SM} Advance & Protect strategy. You might want to think about these moderate-risk strategies as seat belts for your money.

In the three chapters ahead, we'll talk about safe-money investment strategies. These three strategies are fixed index annuities, FIAs with guaranteed income riders, and asset-based long-term care.

CHAPTER 14 TAKEAWAYS:

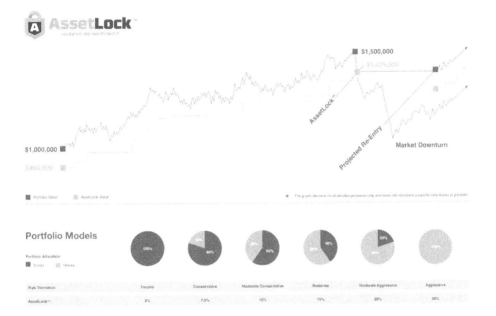

INVESTMENT STRATEGY #6—UPSIDE POTENTIAL WITHOUT DOWNSIDE RISK

FIXED INDEX ANNUITIES (FIAs)

BOND ALTERNATIVE

The reality is that most individuals don't know how to invest their money in safe-money investments today.

Since the bull market in bonds is over and interest rates are so low, people can't afford to put their life savings in the bank to live off of. They need to turn to other investment vehicles.

I understand that money saved in a bank has its place. You need to have a checking account so that you can pay your bills. You need to have a savings account for emergency funds in the event that you need a new roof or water heater for your house, or you need to replace the transmission in your car.

If you lose your job, a rule of thumb in financial planning says you need an emergency fund to help you pay your expenses and sustain your lifestyle for up to six months.

But how about the safe part of your portfolio—the part of your portfolio that's not invested in risk-based or moderate-risk investments? How about the money that you need to generate income off of to sustain your lifestyle in your postretirement years? How are you supposed to invest that money today?

Unfortunately, investing the way our parents or grandparents did may no longer be effective. Investing strictly in bank CDs like the generations before us isn't going to cut it for your retirement at today's interest rates.

Did you realize that you can have guaranteed investment accounts that still have the upside potential earnings for a portion of a stock market index's growth without the downside risk?

By investing your money in a safe-money strategy that has its gains or returns tied to the stock market instead of being tied to interest rates, I believe you'll have a better opportunity to earn the income that you deserve in your retirement.

In my opinion, now is the time to change your mindset away from bonds and into FIAs for a good majority of your nonstock investments. This is the ideal environment for putting some of your money in a fixed index annuity or FIA, which ties your returns to a stock index of some type. Think of the FIA as a bond alternative. You can always go back to the bank or bonds after interest rates get higher like they were in the 1980s. But today, why not tie the rate of return on your fixed money to the stock market instead of interest rates? The stock market has outperformed the bond market two to one for nearly 90 years, according to Ibbotson Associates.

The problem with the stock market is the downside risk to your money. Are you willing to go back to 2008 and 2009 and lose 50 percent again in stocks? Do you remember what that felt like? But what if you could earn stock market gains without losing money when the markets went down? With an FIA, you can participate in some of the upside potential of the stock market without the downside risk.

Today, things are a little bit different in safe-money investing. Fixed index annuities may have a place in your portfolio like you've never thought possible before.

A STRATEGY FOR LONG LIFE

There is a dilemma in this country, a retirement dilemma. That dilemma is the fact that people are living longer than ever and that your money may not last as long as you do.

According to "Income of the Aged Chartbook, 2010," a publication of the Social Security Administration Office of Research, Evaluation, and Statistics, a 65-year-old male has a 9 percent chance of living to age 100, and a 65-year-old female has a 14 percent chance of living to age 100.

The chart below, compiled by JP Morgan Investments for Q1 2015, gives 65-year-old men a 41 percent chance of living to age 90, women an 18 percent chance, and couples a 28 percent chance of at least one of them living to age 90.

In the United States, there is a perceived retirement shortfall of seven years. Imagine running out of money seven years before you die, how would you feel? How stressful would that be? What would you do? Would you move back in with the kids? Obviously, the statistics tell us that we need investments to help our money last as long as we do.

To have guaranteed income for life is a deep longing in the hearts of retirees today. We want to be able to spend our money with confidence because we know that next month's check is coming, and the check after that is coming. Just like Social Security checks just "keep on a comin'," guaranteed income for life from some of your IRA money and even personal savings would be nice—wouldn't it?

PROBABILITY OF REACHING AGES 80 AND 90

Persons aged 65, by gender, and combined couple

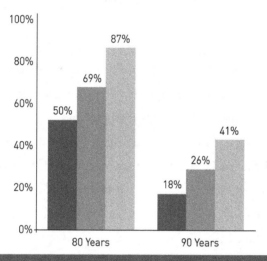

PERCEIVED RETIREMENT SHORTFALL BY COUNTRY

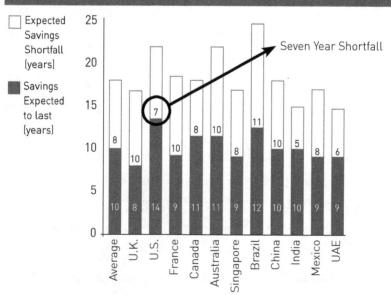

Outliving your money may be a threat to your retirement, and you may need to have some safe-money strategies that keep pace with inflation and your income needs while you live longer than ever.

Contributing to the dilemma is another major issue—the shifting of responsibility for retirement income from the government and corporations to the individual. The burden of funding retirement is overwhelmingly yours today. Whether it's through a 401(k), a 457 deferred compensation plan, or through your own IRAs; you must take a more active role in your retirement than ever before.

WHAT IS A FIXED INDEX ANNUITY?

A fixed index annuity offers returns based on the changes in a securities index, such as the S&P 500® Composite Stock Price Index. Indexed annuity contracts also offer a specified minimum which the contract value will not fall below, regardless of index performance. After a period of time, the insurance company will make payments to you under the terms of your contract. A fixed index annuity is not a stock market investment and does not directly participate in any stock or equity investment. It may be appropriate for individuals who want guaranteed interest rates and the potential for lifetime income. Lifetime income may be provided through the purchase of an optional rider for an additional cost or through annuitization at no additional cost.

It's important to remember, when discussing annuities, that all guarantees and protections are subject to the claims-paying ability of the issuing company.[3]

Fixed index annuities are tax-deferred investment vehicles. Fixed index annuities benefit from triple compounding; you earn interest on your principal, interest on your interest, and interest on the taxes you did not pay. Plus, there's minimal risk of exposure for you as an investor since you earn a percentage of the stock market index growth without the downside risk.

This investment will not expose your hard-earned money to market risk; your principal is protected, and interest gains are systematically credited. A downturn in the index does not reduce your contract value; however, withdrawing assets within a set schedule of time may reduce your principal by fees known as "contingent-deferred sales charge."

While the surrender value of your contract could be less than the purchase payment you put in, some fixed index annuities offer a special minimum value under which the surrender value will not fall.

So you have unlimited growth potential in some fixed indexed growth annuities, a daily tracking of your earnings, riders that can provide guaranteed income for life, and even death benefits for legacy planning that can affect your heirs.

---

3   Nationwide New Heights FIA brochure 2015

HOW DOES IT WORK?

Let's say the stock market grows 10 percent each year for the next five years. That would mean a 50 percent growth in the index over the next five years.

Often, the rider charge or spread cost for the annuity could be 2 to 3 percent per year. So if the spread cost is 2 percent per year, that would mean the cost could be 10 percent to your contract over ten years: 2 percent per year multiplied by five years equals 10 percent. If your gain is 50 percent, and your spread cost was 10 percent, you would've netted 40 percent as a gain, or approximately 8 percent per year for the next five years. Past performance is, of course, no guarantee of future results, and all investments have risks including loss of principal.

Another reduction of gains could be what's called a "cap rate." Some companies put on spread rates with 100 percent participation in an index, and other companies put what's called a cap rate, which means that your index is capped at a certain interest rate, of 3, 4, or 5 percent. If an index is capped at 5 percent, you will earn 5 percent whether the stock market earns 20 percent or 5 percent.

On the plus side, if the stock market loses 20 percent, you may earn nothing. But earning 0 percent in a year that the stock market goes down quickly might be one of the biggest benefits you can have from owning a fixed index annuity.

That's why the FIA works as an investment within the safe-money strategy category—because you can experience some of the upside potential of the stock market without the downside risk.

INVESTING EMOTIONS AND SAFE MARKET STRATEGIES

Safe-money investment strategies are those that are designed to make gains when the stock market is booming and to avoid losses when the market plunges.

If you could remove emotions from the investment equation and make sure that you limit your downside risk, wouldn't you say that you just simplified your financial affairs and helped yourself to at least imagine, if not achieve, financial security for life?

The author of *Stress Free Retirement,* Patrick Kelly, said it's like sitting down at a gambling table to play craps when you know that at that table you'll never lose money, you'll only win. If you could find such a table in Las Vegas, you'd probably keep playing until you fell over exhausted.

The fixed income annuity strategy is similar in concept. When the market goes down you lose nothing, and when the market goes up you have the opportunity to participate in some of its upsides.

Another quote by Patrick Kelly is "It wasn't raining when Noah built the ark." In other words, the right time to take some of the profits off the table and diversify them into other safe-money investment strategies like the FIA is when the markets are up and everything seems to be doing fine.

We believe that a fixed index annuity becomes a very good bond substitute now that the bull market in bonds is over. If you can't receive the return on bonds that you once did (since interest rates are rising and bond values are falling), then why not tie the return of your safe-money investments to the stock market and participate in the upside gains of those less the spread rate, or the cap rate, that would be assessed for your investments?

There are various indexes that can be the engine to drive the growth rate of your returns.

Some indexes are based on the S&P 500, others are based on value stocks, and still others are based on formula-type investments. One of those types of investments is the Case-Shiller index.

A professor at Yale University, Robert Shiller helped pioneer the field of behavioral economics and was recognized for his work with a Nobel Prize in economic science in 2013.

Shiller research has led others to develop an index that helps compensate for the errors sometimes found in behavioral finance. The Case-Shiller index is one that tries to minimize emotions in the equation. You can utilize this Case-Shiller index as one of the indexes that's tied to your fixed index annuity.

Other indexes are put together by world-class banks that invest primarily in dividend-paying stocks. These stocks are actively managed, much like they are in a mutual fund. The investment manager buys and sells dividend-paying stocks according to their investment policy statement. Your money would benefit from the potential gains that are available to dividend-paying stocks.

With interest rates on the rise, and Fed Chairwoman Yellen commenting that she'll continue to raise them in the future, I believe the bull market in bonds is over. If you can't receive the same returns in bonds, then what can you use as a bond alternative? You may want to consider using fixed index annuities as part of that asset class for your money.

ROADBLOCKS AVOIDED

Fixed index annuities may help you reduce stock market losses, because there's limited downside risk. This strategy also helps you overcome the taxes roadblock, because your money grows tax-deferred as long as you leave it in the FIA. You are taxed on the amount of your withdrawals much like you would be in your IRA.

Since some fixed index annuities give you access to the money without any surrender charges in the event that you can't perform two out of six of the activities of daily living or you have a life-threatening illness, they may be an excellent strategy for overcoming the old-age illness roadblock.

The strategy may help you stop procrastinating by allowing you to invest and have participation in stock market gains without the downside risk, even if you put off planning.

This may be the antidote to the roadblock of running out with money. The chassis of the fixed index annuity is built on the insurance company annuity platform, which provides guaranteed income for the rest of your life and possibly for the rest of your spouse's life, if you're married.

Fixed index annuities may help protect you against an unstable economy because your money is safe from the downturns of the stock market, whatever the cause.

There is also a partial hedge against inflation, because the returns on your fixed index annuity are tied to a stock market index of some type, and equities give you a better probability of keeping pace with inflation.

By default, this type of investment is a type of planning, providing you guaranteed income and protecting you against the high cost of long-term care.

ON THE FLIP SIDE

One of the negatives of this type of investment is that you're often required to stay with the product for ten years, much like a ten-year corporate bond or a municipal bond strategy.

If you sold the bond early, you might have to face paying a market value adjustment on your investments. These contracts have a similar market value adjustment and surrender charge if you sell before the ten years is up. So make sure you understand those two numbers: your surrender charge schedule and your potential market value adjustment (MVA) if you surrender the contract during the surrender charge period. Make sure that you have sufficient liquidity in other investments so that the surrender charge period is not an issue.

However, some products give you a free withdrawal of 10 percent every year in the event that you need income along the way. And others allow you to pull out your entire principal through what's called a "return of premium" rider. Caution: Ask your agent how your 10 percent free withdrawals may affect your guaranteed income rider.

One company that we do business with allows you to take out 10 percent the first year, 20 percent the second year, and 100 percent of the value in the third year if you need it or if you just change your mind and decide, for example, that you want to go buy a yacht and travel around the world.

CHAPTER 15 TAKEAWAYS:

FIXED INDEX ANNUITIES

The question with fixed index annuities is this: How much risk are you willing to take? Are you intent on keeping all your money when it comes to safe-money strategies? If you could design your custom-ized fixed index annuity contract, what index would you like to have driving your money? Rank the following indexes in the order of your preference (1 through 5).

_____ S&P index with the blend of a fixed account

_____ Value stock index blended with treasury bills

_____ Nobel Prize-winning Case-Shiller Index

_____ Index tied to commodities including gold, real estate, wheat, and other commodities

_____ Dividend-paying stocks

Which of the two statements gives you the most amount of pain? (Please check only one of the two statements):

_____ I feel more pain when I am *not* fully invested into stocks when the market is going up.

_____ I feel more pain when I am fully invested into stocks during a plunging bear market.

If missing the opportunity on the upside is more painful for you, then you're a growth investor. If it's more painful for you to be invested when the market is dropping, then you're a more conservative investor.

CHAPTER 16

INVESTMENT STRATEGY #7—TAKING GUARANTEED INCOME FOR LIFE

GUARANTEED INCOME RIDERS

In the previous chapter, we talked about the benefits of a fixed index annuity, and this chapter is really devoted to the income riders that you can place on those fixed index annuities. Income riders and other guaranteed riders can provide benefits for you for the rest of your retirement years and possibly for heirs in the event that you die before they do.

FINANCIAL INSURANCE

Do you have fire insurance on your house? If so, why is that? Is it because your house is the largest asset you own? Is it because you can't afford to replace your house if it's destroyed by fire? Do you really want to have a fire so you can collect on your insurance?

While most people never expect to use their fire insurance, they have it nevertheless, because they don't want to go through the devastation of replacing their home and belongings should a fire occur. And if such a disaster does occur, they're very happy that they have the full-replacement-value type of property and casualty insurance.

Having insurance on your safe-money investments such as your fixed index annuities is equally important.

For example, did you know...

- You can get an income rider on a fixed index annuity that may give you guaranteed income for life?
- Some FIAs credit you a bonus in the first year?
- You can purchase some income riders that may even stack up your gains on your index, plus a guaranteed interest rate as well?
- You may qualify for lifetime income for both you and your spouse if you are married?

(Disclaimer: Riders change all the time, so these may not be available at the time of this printing. Also, every product is different, so read the propectus or other material, including the fine print. Understand what you are investing in before investing any money.)

Lifetime withdrawal rates are based on your age at the time you begin taking lifetime income. Some guaranteed income riders increase your lifetime payout if you defer your first paycheck until you are older. By coordinating your guaranteed income rider with the withdrawals you take from your other investments, you may be able to maximize your guaranteed income for life.

If you become unable to perform at least two of six activities of daily living, or ADLs, after you purchase certain types of fixed index annuities, your income rider may allow you to get even more money. This important feature means that you can take out extra income at a time of need. Talk to your agent or retirement advisor and read all materials to understand the details before you invest.

Guaranteed income riders may provide for you a guaranteed bonus and a very generous income to supplement Social Security and cover your fixed expenses. Fixed index annuities may also generate income that's guaranteed for your life and the life of your spouse if you're married. When you pass away, whatever is still left in your FIA will pass on to your listed beneficiary or beneficiaries. Social Security, on the other hand, leaves an empty bag for your heirs when your surviving spouse dies. You must recognize that your principal in a FIA may begin to dwindle over time. If the insurance company is guaranteeing you, let's say, 5 percent income for life and the earnings net of fees and expenses are 3 percent, then your money in a FIA will run out eventually.

Understand that the rider charges are usually assessed on the guaranteed withdrawal amount and not the actual cash value. For example, if you started with $100,000 in your FIA, and because of withdrawals and rider charges your actual cash value is $75,000, your rider charge will be based on the higher of the two numbers. For example, if you are paying a 1 percent rider charge on a $100,000 protected base, that's a fee of $1,000 per year. However, if your cash value is $75,000, then the $1,000 fee is now a much higher percentage. The $1,000 rider charge on $75,000 is now a percentage of 1.3 percent. That's effectively an increase of 33 percent on your fees even though the rider charge is still at 1 percent. If you would like help understanding this more, please talk to your retirement wealth advisor.

Do the fees or the dwindling account value make the FIA a poor investment decision? In my opinion, it may not be a bad choice. Why not? Regardless of where you invest your non-stock money today, you might erode your principal since it may not be earning as much as you withdraw. For example, if you put

$100,000 into the bank and withdraw 5 percent for life, your account value might disappear. Bank savings accounts rarely pay over 1 percent per year today so a 5 percent withdrawal rate will erode your values at a pace of 4 percent per year.

Let's consider short-term investment grade bonds that pay 3 percent per year. This rate of return is not enough to sustain a 5 percent withdrawal rate. With investment grade bonds, your principal value may disintegrate as well.

You may argue that the rates of return for bank accounts and bonds will once again recover back to paying 5 percent or more. First of all, that would be a disaster for our government since we now have $18 trillion of debt and will soon be at $20 trillion of debt. If interest rates return to 5 percent, that means the government will have to pay $1 trillion of interest annually on its teetering mountain of debt. America's budget according to JP Morgan is $3.8 trillion. That means that interest on the debt may become out biggest line item in the budget. Medicare and Medicaid is $948 billion, Social Security is $887 billion, and defense is $609 billion of America's budget according to JP Morgan's quarter 1, 2015 Guide to the Markets.

Anyway, back to your guess that rates will go back up. I would agree with you. But how long will that take? Maybe it will take ten years to get rates back to where you would like them to be. Why not use the upside potential of the stock market without the down side risk until rates are back to normal? Why not invest into a FIA until you are satisfied once again with the interest paid to you on a money market account or investment grade bond or bond fund? In my opinion, using a FIA makes sense as a bond or bank alternative in this low interest rate environment.

ROADBLOCKS AVOIDED

Guaranteed income riders may help avoid the roadblock of stock market losses, because you provide guaranteed income for life and help keep taxes as low as possible.

These riders may also help overcome the old-age illness roadblock, because with some fixed index annuities, you get the potential of a home health care bonus or a substantial increase in income in the event you can't perform two of the six activities of daily living (ADLs). Additional liquidity may also be provided if you can't perform two of the six ADLs or you are affected by a terminal illness of some type.

This strategy bypasses the procrastination roadblock by providing a plan without going out and purchasing long-term care insurance. It may also help overcome the roadblock of running out of money, because it provides guaranteed income that helps supplement your guaranteed Social Security income for life.

Unstable economy roadblocks are bypassed, because the money has a minimum guarantee and a potential participation in the upside of the stock market. Your income is designed to grow over time if you defer taking it or until you stop deferring when you receive that income. These income riders may also help provide an inflation hedge because they are sometimes given a cost-of-living increase over time.

And finally, most people will, by default, create some type of a plan by having this type of an investment. These investments may help you plan for guaranteed income for life.

AS A PENSION SUPPLEMENT

This guaranteed income rider acts like a private pension to help supplement your Social Security or other pension income. Many retirees have found this form of income very helpful in covering fixed expenses, such as mortgages, insurance expenses, taxes, and other fixed standard-of-living expenses.

If you defer taking income out of your guaranteed income rider "private pension," your potential guaranteed income for life may increase as you get older. Check your prospectus, sales brochures, illustrations, company websites, and other literature to nail down the details about your FIA benefits.

Once again, products vary, and the numbers constantly change because products constantly change. To ensure that your income flow is truly *guaranteed for life* by the money you invest into a guaranteed income rider, make sure you have that in writing from the issuing insurance company.

THE EXPENSES

Most of these contracts do not charge a front-end load or commission, but they do have a penalty, typically for approximately ten years if you surrender the entire contract. There's also the market value adjustment (MVA) during that ten-year period. Below is an example of a ten-year contingent deferred sales charge (CDSC) schedule:

1	2	3	4	5	6	7	8	9	10
14%	12%	10%	8%	7%	6%	6%	5%	4 %	3%

Beware that there may also be a market value adjustment (MVA) if you surrender your FIA before the CDSC is expired. During this period, you may have access to a 10 percent free withdrawal during an emergency.

The easiest way to explain how a MVA works is that it is similar to selling a ten-year bond out of your portfolio before it matures. If you buy a ten-year bond and interest rates continue to go up, you could receive less than what you invested if you sell the bond before maturity. This is similar to an MVA, because the higher interest rate may cause the bond values to drop.

Other costs to the investment include the spread rate, which may be 3 percent or more, and the cost of the rider, which may be 1.0 percent or more annually.

As you can see, you must be comfortable with this particular investment's long-term commitment. You need to have other investments that are completely liquid (such as AssetLock, Welshire^{SM} Advance & Protect, mutual funds, stocks, or ETFs), so that you can access them when needed. Consider this investment an income generator that may not provide any money at the end of your life to pass to heirs, but in the event you die too soon, whatever is left in the contract goes to your heirs. Unlike Social Security, where none of your principal passes to your heirs upon death, 100 percent of what's left in this investment could potentially pass on to your beneficiaries.

CHAPTER 17

INVESTMENT STRATEGY #8— OLD-AGE ILLNESS INSURANCE

ASSET-BASED LONG-TERM CARE

Isn't it true that paying for health care may be your largest expense in your postretirement years, especially if you develop an old-age illness, which most people do at some point? That's the unfortunate truth; there's a very good chance you'll eventually develop an old-age illness that will lead to death.

Doesn't it make sense then to create a path for the retirement you worked so hard for? Whether your dreams include relaxing with your family, enjoying your favorite hobbies or sports, or working with a charity, you need to have some type of plan to help you pay for the high cost of long-term care.

In order to answer questions like "Do I have enough," "Will I run out," "Am I on track?" you need to put together a retirement wealth plan to see if you are indeed on track. This retirement wealth plan may include direction for estate and tax planning, asset protection, and investment management. When you're not at work earning money, then you need your money to be at work earning money.

The income that you earn off your investments may help provide your standard of living in your postretirement years.

Consider the expenses you'll have during your retirement years: fixed expenses include taxes, medical insurance, utilities, and so on, while consistent expenses include fuel for your vehicle, food, clothing, entertainment, and gifts. Why not create a guaranteed income stream to provide income for those guaranteed fixed expenses? And why not tie the return of those investments to the stock market instead of tying them to bank rates or interest rates?

Safe-money strategies may help provide guaranteed income for life, which could result in you fulfilling your dream of having lifetime financial security and having greater peace in your soul.

Since retirement is also the time in life when you begin to face the threat of old-age illness, as you consider safe-money strategies you should also think about the high cost of long-term care and some new strategies that may help protect your money and keep it in your family for years to come.

CD ALTERNATIVES

Do you remember when you'd open a savings account or CD and the bank would give you a toaster? Well, today there are no free toasters for new bank accounts, and there are few rewards for opening a CD. In fact, it seems we might be paying more in fees than we are receiving in interest these days.

CDs, once known as certificates of deposit, sometimes seem more aptly named "certificates of depreciation" when you take the taxes out of the interest on the CD and adjust it for inflation these days. Investment analysts on Wall Street may call this type of investment "going broke safely." Your interest rate minus taxes and inflation equals a loss.

If all of your money were in a bank earning 0.5 percent, did you realize it would take you 20 years to grow your money by 10 percent? To keep pace with inflation today, you need to look beyond the traditional checking account, savings account, or CDs at a bank.

You also need to look at investments outside of government and investment-grade bonds. There's just not enough interest paid today on investments to be able to sustain a guaranteed interest rate for your money.

Think about it this way, your bank account is in your right pocket. What if you could transfer your money from your right pocket to your left pocket and receive no less interest on your money but get tax deferral? What if the money you moved over to your left pocket might double when you die? What if you were healthy enough to qualify for the money in your left pocket to double, triple, or even quadruple when you have to begin receiving long-term care benefits such as assisted living?

Asset-based long-term care policies may help you work toward achieving those goals. By moving a little bit of your money from the right pocket to the left, you just might add some more value to your retirement wealth plan.

THE HIGH COST OF LONG-TERM CARE

In an earlier chapter we talked about Genworth's Cost of Care Survey app, which contains data from more than 14,800 long-term care providers across the United States.

By pulling up the data for my location, La Crosse, Wisconsin, I found staggering costs associated with long-term care ($49,192 a year for a home health aide, $15,288 for adult day care, $30,000 for an assisted-living facility, and $82,855 for skilled care).

With those extremely high costs, you can see that it wouldn't take long for all of your money to be consumed by the high cost of long-term care.

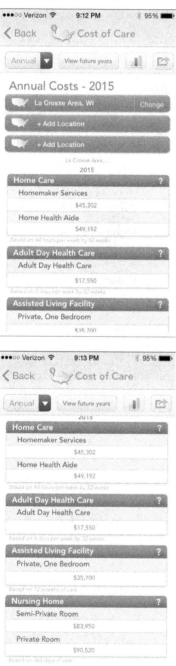

So what can a person do to protect their assets?

There are three general strategies that are very popular among retirees today: asset-based long-term care, asset-protection trust for Medicaid, and an asset-protection trust for veteran's benefits.

ASSET-BASED LONG-TERM CARE STRATEGY

Under the Pension Protection Act of 2006, new strategies were developed to help you avoid the ridiculously high increases in premiums that insurance companies are charging for long-term care.

In the past, you would pay a long-term care premium to get your coverage on an annual basis. Each year, the insurance company would tell you what that premium would be; it was a little like health insurance, essentially a rent-as-you-go policy. If you didn't make your payment that year, you'd lose your coverage.

Since in retirement the threat of old-age illness is upon you permanently, you need a long-term solution.

One permanent solution might be an asset-based long-term care strategy.

For example, if Mary, who's age 65 and in good health, deposited $50,000 into an asset-preservation strategy combo life and long-term care, she could receive an income tax reduction benefit of approximately $100,000 upon death and a possible leverage on her long-term care benefits of around $200,000. So by using $50,000 for long-term care costs, Mary could double her investment for a death benefit and nearly quadruple her investment to receive long-term care insurance if her health is good. Mary's investment of $50,000 may provide about $200,000 of long-term care insurance that would cover a lot of years in an assisted-living facility. (Please refer back to page 41 for a diagram of asset-based long-term care insurance.)

Let's say Mary's receiving $15,000 per year of Social Security, and she has to come up with an additional $15,000 to pay for her total annual cost of $30,000 for assisted living. If she has $200,000 that can be used to pay for that care, divided by $15,000 a year, she can afford just over 13 years of coverage. If she went into a skilled care facility where the cost of a semi-private room is $82,855, she needs to come up with $67,855 per year. So $200,000 divided by $67,855 is just under three years of coverage.

This would at least give her three years where she could begin to create an additional gifting strategy. If she had to stay another couple of years, that fourth and fifth year of her expenses would have to be covered by other assets. Then, if she were to gift money away as soon as she goes into a long-term care facility and let her asset-based long-term care coverage and her Social Security pay for her care, she could preserve that gifted money except for those two years that were not covered by her asset-based long-term care.

Her solution would be to raise the amount of money she puts into her asset-based long-term care. In this case, she would need, under the current rule, five years of coverage. That would be $339,275 of long-term care benefits ($67,855 multiplied by five years). She'd still need to put in about $84,819 to secure that coverage if her leverage was four times her premium ($339,275 divided by four equals about $84,819).

If Mary is not healthy, she could qualify for another form of asset-based long-term care strategy called an annuity-based long-term care strategy. In this example, Mary could take an old fixed annuity contract and roll it into an annuity-based long-term care strategy, the new kind of annuity, which could give her up to $420,000 of long-term care. She could take advantage of this type of strategy with only a simplified medical questionnaire.

Finally, a strategy that's growing in popularity is to use IRA money to purchase long-term care.

To illustrate this strategy, let's look at Tim, who's age 60 and has a $500,000 IRA. By repositioning $157,000 of his IRA account into a lifetime long-term care policy funded with an IRA-based annuity over a 20-year period, he could receive a lifetime long-term care monthly benefit of $5,367. This allows him to maintain $343,000 and receive a death benefit of $268,345.

The aforementioned example is taken from the book *Don't Go Broke in a Nursing Home*, by Don Quante, which adds that:

> *This type of IRA-based long-term care policy is unique*
> *in the sense that it starts out as an IRA annuity policy,*

also known as a tax-qualified annuity, and then over a 20-year period makes equal distribution internally to the insurance carrier and funds the life insurance. The owner of the IRA annuity will receive annually for 20 years a 1099-R (the IRS form that reports the taxable amount of an IRA distribution) on the amount of the IRA that's moved annually to fund the life insurance policy.

In another of the book's examples, Tim is widowed and comfortably retired, but he's concerned about how to pay for long-term care. "Like many people his age, he has what we call 'qualified money rich … nonqualified poor.' In other words, Tim has a lot more IRA-type money (before tax) than he does after-tax money."

In Tim's case, the solution is to take advantage of a "tax-free trustee-to-trustee transfer" by repositioning the $157,000 into an IRA-based annuity to fund a life policy that will in turn provide Tim with a pool of money for the long term.

This creates a death benefit of $268,335 payable upon his death to his children while providing a monthly benefit of $5,367 for long-term care needs such as home health, assisted living, adult daycare, or skilled nursing care.

To summarize, instead of paying annual premiums for your long-term care insurance that may experience 20–50 percent of premium increases without warning, why not consider using an asset-based long-term care strategy where you never have to pay another annual premium?

Transferring money from one pocket to the other, from a taxable pocket to a tax-free pocket, can ensure that you have tax-free money to use for the high cost of long-term care if you need it. Then, if you don't need it, that tax-free death benefit goes to your heirs at a higher level than what you deposited, up to 200 percent of the deposit that you put in.

Those who do not qualify because of health may still be able to qualify for the simplified issue annuity-based long-term care strategy. These strategies and others can be explored with a retirement wealth advisor.

ASSET-PROTECTION TRUST FOR MEDICAID

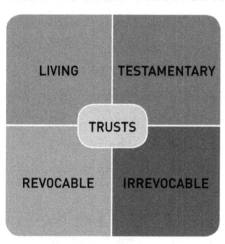

In the late 1980s, the late attorney John Bosshard joined me on WKTY's "Brent Welch Talks Money" radio program. He told the listening audience that all trusts are split into four areas: living (inter vivos), testamentary, revocable, and irrevocable.

The second strategy for protecting assets from the high cost of long-term care is the asset-protection trust for Medicaid, which is an irrevocable living trust. Using Don Quante's definition:

> *An irrevocable trust is an arrangement in which the grantor departs with ownership and control of property.*
>
> *Usually, this involves a gift of the property to the trust. The trust then stands as a separate taxable entity and pays tax on its accumulated income. Trusts typically receive a deduction for income that is distributed on a current basis. Because the grantor must permanently depart with the ownership and control of the property being transferred*

into the irrevocable trust, such a device has limited appeal to many taxpayers.

Homes that have been put into an irrevocable trust are generally not eligible for a reverse mortgage. An irrevocable trust is typically used in very advanced estate planning strategies.

Essentially, the way to use Medicaid to pay for long-term care is to put money into an irrevocable trust and then establish Medicaid eligibility, which protects the assets in the trust.

For example, if a couple puts $100,000 from a money market along with $48,000 from their checking account into an irrevocable trust, Medicaid eligibility could be established after a penalty period (which in this example is 34.5 months). The $148,000 would then be asset protected. Tax must be paid on income from very high level trusts; the trustee can distribute the income to the beneficiary, which is likely to be a surviving spouse or heirs such as children or grandchildren.

The assets in the irrevocable asset-protection trust for Medicaid could be invested in a tax-deferred strategy as well or a tax-free strategy so that your money grows in a tax-advantaged environment.

Here's a quick story to illustrate how this asset-protection trust for Medicaid works: Lisa transferred $80,000 into this type of trust, and shortly afterward her husband developed Alzheimer's and ended up in a specialized unit of a skilled long-term care facility. Although the cost of his care ended up spending down a good portion of her assets, as the unaffected spouse she was able to keep the value of her IRA, various assets, and $115,920. Lisa had one regret, that she didn't put more money into her irrevocable trust when she was able to. She didn't give more to the irrevocable trust because she didn't want to lose control. In the end, she discovered that she lost control by not putting the money in an irrevocable trust. If she was able to do it over, she would have chosen to keep more control by putting more money into the irrevocable trust.

Your assets can be split into exempt, countable, and unavailable assets and categorized before creating a strategy that may help protect your assets. An irrevocable trust can help protect your assets from creditors and from the creditors of your children's estate as well.

The way the Medicaid rules work is that, if you apply for Medicaid, the government goes back five years to look for any gifts given. If a gift was given within that five-year period, it may delay the point at which you begin to receive Medicaid benefits. Talk to your attorney for specific information about protecting what's yours through irrevocable trusts.

DISCLAIMER: The author is not an attorney, accountant or CPA but addresses these issues as a Certified Financial Planning Practitioner®. The author advises that you do not try to do these strategies yourself. Seek the help of an elder care attorney, VA benefits specialist, and an estate-planning attorney to help you with your planning and to draft your documents.

ASSET-PROTECTION TRUST FOR VETERAN'S BENEFITS

The third strategy to protect your assets from the high cost of long-term care is an asset-protection trust for veteran's benefits.

A largely unknown benefit offered by the Veteran's Administration is a special pension with an "aid-and-attendance" benefit. Through this benefit, veterans and their spouses can receive monetary assistance in paying for someone to assist with eating, bathing, dressing, and other needs.

The benefit is available for veterans who were honorably discharged after serving at least one day during a defined period of war (World War I, World War II, Korea, Vietnam, and the Persian Gulf Crisis), and the benefit is not dependent on a service-related injury.

A tax advisor can let you know if you qualify for the monthly aid of up to $2,054 per month for a couple, $1,732 for a veteran, or $1,113 for a surviving spouse.

There is no five-year lookback for assets transferred to an asset-protection veteran's administration trust, so if you qualify under the income and asset rules for the Veteran's Administration benefits, then these trusts might protect your money for your heirs and help you receive over $24,000 a year of tax-free money to help pay for the high cost of long-term care.

Wouldn't it be nice to receive an additional $24,000 tax free to be used toward the cost of your long-term care?

OTHER ASPECTS

The only real downside of an asset-based long-term care strategy is that you're typically putting money aside in a more permanent place that's not as liquid. Some contracts allow you to take 100 percent of the money out after the first year; others only allow for a 10 percent free withdrawal during the start period, typically ten years long. So you give up liquidity—that's a negative—and you give up the ability to invest that money in the stock market because it's in a guaranteed strategy.

If you don't use this strategy once it's set up, you do not lose it. It moves on a tax-free basis to your heirs through the death benefit provisions. If you put $50,000 in, your heirs might get $100,000. The death benefit would leverage up to two times, and the asset-based long-term care benefits could be a tax-free benefit of up to four times the deposit.

ROADBLOCKS AVOIDED

An asset-based long-term care strategy addresses the stock market losses roadblock, because it's not invested in the stock market at all. It also addresses the tax issues roadblock, because you're taking taxable money and moving it into tax-free strategies to be used either for long-term care or as a tax-free death benefit. It's a tax-deferred, if not tax-free strategy.

This strategy also covers the high cost of old-age illness and long-term care associated with that. It helps people coordinate their estate planning with their long-term care planning. May I ask you a question? Have you been putting off your estate planning and long-term care planning for years or even decades? It is time to overcome the procrastinating roadblock and see your retirement wealth advisor and elder care/estate planning attorney today.

As for the running out of money roadblock, this strategy might provide up to 400 percent leverage to cover the high-cost long-term care. Therefore, it leverages your money and may help keep you from running out of your other money, because you're using the insurance company's money leveraged on top of your money to pay the bills.

As guaranteed-type products, asset-based long-term care strategies may help overcome the unstable economy roadblock. People tend to dislike insurance companies because they always win. Instead of hating insurance companies because they always seem to make money at your expense, why not love them because they always make money? Why not use the insurance company's profitability to your advantage by creating an asset-based long-term care strategy? Why not use that stability to underwrite your personal economy and bring you more confidence and peace about your asset-protection plan?

As for the inflation roadblock, this strategy leverages your money to help keep pace with inflation, and you can put inflation riders on these policies to keep pace with inflation. This strategy can also be a remedy for the no plan roadblock.

In the Appendix section of this book, you'll find a Welshire^{SM} Capital Confidential Personal and Financial Profile. Fill this out to get an asset protection strategy designed just for you.

Now that we've discussed the eight roadblocks and the Eight Investment Strategies for Life, let's look at some general investment truths.

CHAPTER 17 TAKEAWAYS:

*RISK THERMOMETER FOR 8 INVESTMENT STRATEGIES FOR LIFE (**SEMI AUTO**)*

RISKY

S Stocks

E ETFs

M Mutual funds

Target rate of return hoped for (not guaranteed or projected): 7-10%*
100% stocks, potential inflation hedge and growth

MODERATE

I Investment air bags

A AssetLock or Welshire[SM] Advance and Protect

Target rate of return hoped for (not guaranteed or projected) 5% -6%*

0 to 100% stocks, tactical strategies with some VA guaranteed income potential, potential protection from market volatility and unstable economy.

SAFE

U   Upside potential without downside risk

T   Taking guaranteed income for life

O   Old-age illness insurance

FIAs, FIAs with income riders and Asset-Based LTCi

Target return hoped for 0% - 4%

0% stocks, guaranteed by the general assets of underlying insurance company, potential guaranteed income for life, protection from stock market volatility, unstable economy, and old-age illnesses.

*All investments have risk including the loss of principle. Past performance is no guarantee of future results. This is not meant to be a projection or expectation. Because of the higher risk, these returns could be negative for extended periods of time.

CHAPTER 18

THE THREE CIRCLES OF FINANCE

PLANNING BETWEEN THE TAX LINES

One of my mentors since I started in the business in August 1984 was John Savage, an early pioneer in financial planning who gave a brilliant and simple explanation of how money works between the tax lines.

During his workshops, he would draw on his whiteboard three circles that he labeled "taxable," "tax deferred," and "tax free." Then he would ask the audience, "Which investments fit in each of those circles?" "If you had a list of investments such as money markets, CDs, bonds, mutual funds, stocks, ETFs, annuities, 401(k)s, IRAs, ROTH IRAs, municipal bonds, what circle would you put each investment into?"

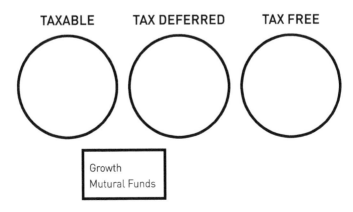

Usually he'd start by asking, "How about the taxable circle?" to which someone would answer, "Well, money markets fit in there," and someone else would say, "CDs fit in there," and another person would reply, "Bonds fit in there."

Then John would say, "How about tax-deferred investments? What investments fit in that circle?" Somebody would say, "Stocks go there," and someone else would add, "Exchange-traded funds."

Then, someone would suggest "IRAs," and that would open up a world of discussion about how qualified plans such as 403(b), 401(k), profit-sharing, and pension plans for large and small companies fit in the tax-deferred circle.

Now, I like to add a box between the taxable and the tax-deferred circles. In that box, I like to insert mutual funds. This is where you would place a balanced mutual fund that has some taxable characteristics, and that also has some tax-deferred characteristics, which occurs if the underlying stocks are not sold and you still maintain some unrealized capital gains. In other words, mutual funds are a type of hybrid between taxable and tax-deferred investments.

In his discussion, John would then ask people in the audience, "What fits under tax-free investments?" Someone might say, "Municipal bonds fit in that circle," while someone else might add "Roth IRAs," and another audience member might say, "Roth 401(k) plans."

The three circles of finance are used to categorize investments that you currently own. They are also used to help you reduce your overall tax burden by moving some of your money between the tax lines. For example, you could move some money from CDs over to IRAs or Roth IRAs to get tax-deferred growth today and potential tax-free withdrawals down the road.

But John would always add, "When you file your taxes every year, you have a schedule where all your tax dollars show up. On that tax schedule, you pay tax on all your taxable investments, and you list the amounts of taxes you pay and the source from the funds that generated those 1099s that add up to the taxes you put on your tax return." Imagine if you could stop the flow of some of your 1099s and keep your taxes as low as possible. The three circles of finance may help you visualize the tax characteristics of your current investments and how to reposition them in order to create a better tax plan.

THE RELEVANCE OF THE THREE CIRCLES

What you need to understand is that all the investments that you currently own fit into one of John's three circles of finance.

The key to keeping your taxes as low as possible is to move your money between the tax lines from one circle to another. For example, by converting your IRA to a Roth IRA, you're moving your money from the tax-deferred circle to the tax-free circle.

I mentioned in a previous chapter about how I ask attendees of my workshops whether they think taxes are going up or going down. The answer, of course, is that taxes are inevitably going to go up.

So if taxes are going up in the future, where would you want most all of your money to be? People would probably say, "Well, the tax-free circle." Ideally, that would be correct: Put as much of your investments as you can in the tax-free circle, which means you should max out your Roth IRAs and your Roth 401(k)s.

But one point that needs to be understood is that your tax-deferred investments will become taxable when you sell them.

For example, if you bought an apartment building that cost $100,000, and you later sold it for $200,000, you would have to pay capital gains tax on the $100,000 gain. Or, if you depreciated it and you have no basis left, you might have to pay tax on the full $200,000.

If you held that investment until you died, the day you die you get a step up in basis from capital gains tax. If you die in a marital property state like Wisconsin, and you've created survivorship marital property out of it, you can get a double step up in basis and sanitize the tax-deferred assets that are held outside of an IRA from taxes.

You can work toward paying no capital gains taxes on those assets, such as highly appreciated stocks, ETFs, mutual funds, or real estate. Your estate tax is your tax on your right to die in America. There is an estate tax on the federal level, and many states have an estate tax. Wisconsin does not currently have an estate tax, but Minnesota does. Understand the tax laws in the state you live in so that you can keep your taxes as low as possible. You need to have quite a substantial estate to pay estate taxes at the federal level in 2015, $5.43 million, but in Minnesota, the state estate tax starts at $1.4 million in 2015. Consult your tax adviser or CPA for all the current details for your state.

Almost everybody's estate is subject to probate. In addition to keeping taxes low, you can also keep the fees of probate low through proper planning.

To keep your capital gains taxes and estate taxes as low as possible, it is in your best interest to understand how your investments fit in your estate plan and how you can match the assets you own to the strategies in your estate plan.

In summary, the three circles of finance may help you identify the tax characteristics of every investment you own. Once those tax characteristics are identified, you can work toward keeping taxes as low as possible by moving assets from the taxable to the tax-deferred circle or from the taxable to the tax-free circle.

INVESTMENT TYPE	TAXABLE	TAX-DEFERRED	TAX-FREE
Money market	X		
Checking account	X		
CDs	X		
Corporate bonds	X		
Muni-bonds			X
Roth IRAs			X
Roth 401(k)s			X
401(k)s		X	
IRAs		X	
Annuities		X	
Stocks	X	X	
Mutual funds	X	X	
ETFs	X	X	

THE MAGICAL DOUBLING DOLLAR

To illustrate the power of tax deferral over time, I'm turning to best-selling author Patrick Kelly and his book *Stress-Free Retirement*. In it, he uses the example of the "magical doubling dollar" to illustrate what would happen if you start with a dollar and double it every year over 20 years.

THE MAGIC DOUBLING DOLLAR

	$1
	$2
	$4
	$8
	$16
	$32

HOW MUCH DO WE HAVE AFTER THE 20TH DOUBLE?

How much do you end up with after the 20th tax-deferred double? It's a whopping $1,048,576!

Now take that same dollar and apply a 25 percent tax on the gain every time it doubles. The end result? Only $72,570 and change.

Few people are going to earn a 100 percent return every year for 20 years, which is what it takes to double the money, but these charts do amplify the dramatic effect that taxes have on a person's investment return.

It's also important, once you retire, to consolidate and simplify your tax-deferred investments. For example, you may decide to transfer your 401(k), SEP plan, and 457 deferred compensation plan into an IRA.

We did this for one client, who in fact had 21 IRAs that we consolidated into just several IRAs and Roth IRAs; a few of each for each spouse.

This demonstrates how the individual investor can experience the freedom of simplifying their investments within each of the tax circles.

CHAPTER 18 TAKEAWAYS:

ROLLOVER CHART

1/23/2015

Roll From	Roll To							
	Roth IRA	Traditional IRA	SIMPLE IRA	SEP-IRA	Governmental 457(b)	Qualified Plan[1] (pre-tax)	403(b) (pre-tax)	Designated Roth Account (401(k), 403(b) or 457(b))
Roth IRA	YES[2]	NO	NO	NO	NO	NO	NO	NO
Traditional IRA	YES[3]	YES[2]	NO	YES[2]	YES[4]	YES	YES	NO
SIMPLE IRA	YES,[3] after two years	YES,[2] after two years	YES[2]	YES,[2] after two years	YES,[4] after two years	YES, after two years	YES, after two years	NO
SEP-IRA	YES[3]	YES[2]	NO	YES[2]	YES[4]	YES	YES	NO
Governmental 457(b)	YES[3]	YES	NO	YES	YES	YES	YES	YES[3,5]
Qualified Plan[1] (pre-tax)	YES[3]	YES	NO	YES	YES[4]	YES	YES	YES[3,5]
403(b) (pre-tax)	YES[3]	YES	NO	YES	YES[4]	YES	YES	YES[3,5]
Designated Roth Account (401(k), 403(b) or 457(b))	YES	NO	NO	NO	NO	NO	NO	YES[6]

[1] Qualified plans include, for example, profit-sharing, 401(k), money purchase and defined benefit plans
[2] Only one rollover in any 12-month period
[3] Must include in income
[4] Must have separate accounts
[5] Must be an in-plan rollover
[6] Any amounts distributed must be rolled over via direct (trustee-to-trustee) transfer to be excludable from income
For more information regarding retirement plans and rollovers, visit Tax Information for Retirement Plans.

CHAPTER 19

TRUE WEALTH

"WHEREVER YOUR TREASURE IS... YOUR HEART WILL ALSO BE." (MATT. 6:21 NLT)

Imagine taking your smartphone out of your pocket and finding your time travel app on your screen. Launching the app, you close your eyes and travel back in time once again.

This time, you set the dial to travel back more than 2,000 years to the days of Jesus. You're going to eavesdrop and listen in on what Jesus said to three different people about true wealth.

First we'll listen in on a conversation Jesus had with the rich young ruler, then we'll watch him interact with the woman at the well, and finally we'll feel what Nicodemus felt when Jesus talked to him about the $1 billion asset transfer.

TIME TRAVEL APP

THE RICH MAN

Let's watch Jesus as he talks to the rich young ruler about true wealth. During this conversation, Jesus wanted to find out where the rich young ruler stored up his treasure. Of course, Jesus knew where the rich young ruler's heart was, but he wanted the man to discover where his true wealth was stored: Did he store it on Earth or in heaven? Jesus made his view on true wealth clear when he said, "Don't store up treasures here on earth, where moths eat them and rust destroys them, and where thieves break in and steal. Store your treasures in heaven, where moths and rust cannot destroy, and thieves do not break in and steal" (Matthew 6:19–20 NLT).

Jesus wanted the rich young ruler to check his own heart; he wanted him to experience freedom from the gravitational pull of wealth.

Let's pick up the story in Mark's account in the New Testament:

> As Jesus was starting out on his way to Jerusalem, a man came running up to him, knelt down, and asked, "Good Teacher, what must I do to inherit eternal life?"
>
> "Why do you call me good?" Jesus asked. "Only God is truly good. But to answer your question, you know the commandments: You must not murder. You must not commit adultery. You must not steal. You must not testify falsely. You must not cheat anyone. Honor your father and mother."
>
> "Teacher," the man replied, "I've obeyed all these commandments since I was young."
>
> Looking at the man, Jesus felt genuine love for him. "There is still one thing you haven't done," he

told him. "Go and sell all your possessions and give the money to the poor, and you will have treasure in heaven. Then come, follow me." At this, the man's face fell, and he went away sad, for he had many possessions.

You see, true wealth is what money can't buy and death can't take away. This rich man had a huge house, a boss car, a plump and overflowing 401(k) plan, multiple businesses, millions in dividend-paying blue-chip stocks, and cash-flowing real estate. His treasure was here on Earth, and the desires of his heart were here, too.

"No one can serve two masters. For you will hate one and love the other; you will be devoted to one and despise the other. You cannot serve both God and money" (Matthew 6:24).

Jesus wants to bless you, to provide and protect you, to help you. He is for you! After all, since God didn't spare even his own son but gave him up for you, won't he also give you everything else? (Romans 8:32)

It's not that He hates money; He just doesn't want us to love money.

No, money isn't the root of all evil; the love of money is the root of all kinds of evil. (1 Timothy 6:10)

Let's finish up with this story:

Jesus looked around and said to his disciples, "How hard it is for the rich to enter the Kingdom of God! In fact, it is easier for a camel to go through the eye of a needle than for a rich person to enter the Kingdom of God!"

The disciples were astounded. "Then who in the world can be saved?" they asked.

Jesus looked at them intently and said, "Humanly speaking, it is impossible. But not with God. Everything is possible with God" (Mark 10:17-23, 25-27 NLT).

THE WOMAN AT THE WELL

Water makes up 71 percent of the Earth's surface and up to 60 percent of our bodies. According to the US Geological Survey (usgs.gov), the brain and the heart are composed of 73 percent water, and the lungs are about 83 percent water. The skin contains 64 percent water, and muscles and kidneys are 79 percent water.

When Jesus talked about water, he was talking about one of our most-needed substances. We can only live for a week without water, but we can go for more than three weeks without food. According to Business Insider (www.businessinsider.com), Claude Piantadosi of Duke University told Fox, "You can go 100 hours without drinking at an average temperature outdoors."

Jesus talked to the woman at the well about the importance of a different kind of water—living water. This living water will help you never be thirsty again. Once you taste of this living water you will be eternally satisfied in a way you never thought possible. Let's experience the endless supply of living water that Jesus talked about.

Now, take out your smartphone and launch your time travel app once more. Close your eyes and travel back to see and hear Jesus as he interacts with the woman at the well.

Here's the story from the Bible:

Jesus, tired from the long walk, sat wearily beside the well about noontime. Soon a Samaritan woman came to draw water, and Jesus said to her, "Please give me a drink." He was alone at the time because his disciples had gone into the village to buy some food.

The woman was surprised, for Jews refuse to have anything to do with Samaritans. She said to Jesus, "You are a Jew, and I am a Samaritan woman. Why are you asking me for a drink?'

Jesus replied, "If you only knew the gift God has for you and who you are speaking to, you would ask me, and I would give you living water."

"But sir, you don't have a rope or a bucket," she said, "and this well is very deep. Where would you get this living water? And besides, do you think you're greater than our ancestor Jacob, who gave us this well? How can you offer better water than he and his sons and his animals enjoyed?"

Jesus replied, "Anyone who drinks this water will soon become thirsty again. But those who drink the water I give will never be thirsty again. It becomes a fresh, bubbling spring within them, giving them eternal life."

"Please, sir," the woman said, "give me this water! Then I'll never be thirsty again, and I won't have to come here to get water."

Jesus replied, "But the time is coming—indeed it's here now—when true worshipers will worship the Father in spirit and in truth. The Father is looking for those who will worship Him that way. For God is Spirit, so those who worship Him must worship in spirit and in truth."

The woman said, "I know the Messiah is coming—the one who is called Christ. When he comes, he will explain everything to us."

Then Jesus told her, "I AM the Messiah!" (John 4:6-15, 23-26 NLT)

NICODEMUS

Now let's see if you can feel what Nicodemus felt when he spoke with Jesus. This is from John, chapter three of the Bible:

There was a man named Nicodemus, a Jewish religious leader who was a Pharisee. After dark one evening, he came to speak with Jesus.

"Rabbi," he said, "we all know that God has sent you to teach us. Your miraculous signs are evidence that God is with you."

Jesus replied, "I tell you the truth, unless you are born again, you cannot see the Kingdom of God."

"What do you mean?" exclaimed Nicodemus. "How can an old man go back into his mother's womb and be born again?"

Jesus replied, "I assure you, no one can enter the Kingdom of God without being born of water and the Spirit. Humans can reproduce only human life, but the Holy Spirit gives birth to spiritual life. So don't be surprised when I say, 'You must be born again.' The wind blows wherever it wants. Just as you can hear the wind but can't tell where it comes from or where it is going, so you can't explain how people are born of the Spirit."

"How are these things possible?" Nicodemus asked.

Jesus replied, "You are a respected Jewish teacher, and yet you don't understand these things? I assure you, we tell you what we know and have seen, and yet you won't believe our testimony. But if you don't believe me when I tell you about earthly things, how can you possibly believe if I tell you about heavenly things? No one has ever gone to heaven and returned. But the Son of Man has come down from heaven."

"For this is how God loved the world: He gave his one and only Son, so that everyone who believes in Him will not perish but have eternal life. God sent his Son into the world not to judge the world, but to save the world through Him" (John 3:1–13, 16–17 NLT).

Imagine that God gives you a $1 billion tax-free deposit in your bank account today. All you have to do is write checks on that account for all of your temporal and spiritual needs. Wouldn't that be cool? A billion dollars would make us all feel rich! God sent his son Jesus for you and me in order to bless us with a $1 billion gift—spiritually speaking. This $1 billion makes you a spiritual billionaire with all the riches of heaven.

You see, when you believe in Jesus you will not perish but will have eternal life. When you believe that Jesus died and shed his blood to forgive your sins, He can live in you and through you. You will be born again. When you have that spiritual new birth, all the riches of heaven are yours through Christ: You become a new creation, old things pass away and all things become new.

When you believe in Jesus, you are drinking up the living water, and you will never thirst again. You are a child of God, a co-heir with Christ, and all the riches of heaven that were poured out into Christ are now yours. Christ in you is your hope of glory! It's like you hit the mother lode of jackpots for your life. You are a spiritual billionaire and greatly blessed, highly favored, and deeply loved.

Don't be like the rich young ruler whose trust was purely in earthly wealth. Choose to store up riches in heaven—true wealth that money can't buy and death can't take away! If you seek first the Kingdom of God and if you believe in Jesus, you will discover true wealth.

"Seek the Kingdom of God above all else, and live righteously, and he will give you everything you need" (Matthew 6:33 NLT).

CHAPTER 19 TAKEAWAYS:

*MY FRIEND GREG STRAND, EXECUTIVE DIRECTOR OF
THEOLOGY AND CREDENTIALING AT THE EVANGELICAL
FREE CHURCH OF AMERICA, EFCA.ORG READ THIS CHAPTER
AND WROTE THE FOLLOWING SUMMARY FOR YOU.*

As Augustine stated about our fallen state, our hearts are restless
until they find rest in God. The true treasure is Jesus Christ. This
treasure consists of both His person and His message: the gospel
of Jesus Christ. The gospel must be believed and received (Jn. 1:12).
An integral part of that message and response is repentance, which
is a turning from and a turning to. When Jesus came preaching
the kingdom, where the true treasures are found, he proclaimed,
"The time is fulfilled, and the kingdom of God is at hand; repent and
believe in the gospel" (Mk. 1:15). The kingdom of God is our first
priority and when that is true all God's other blessings are ours as
well (Matt. 6:19-20, 33-34). This treasure is such that one is willing to
sell all to obtain all (Matt. 13:44). As an example of one who believed
and received, upon encountering Jesus Zacchaeus' whole life was
changed and it was first made evident in the way he handled earthly
possessions (Lk. 19:2-10). As a contrary example, the rich man
concluded that life existed in his wealth and possessions and he did
all he could to retain it all (Lk. 12:15-21). In the end, he lost it all, for
eternity. What about you?

ACTION PLAN:
As we close up this book and think about true wealth that money
can't buy and death can't take away, we have to consider our
spiritual life. The core of our being can be filled up with the Holy
Spirit of God. When you believe in Jesus, you transfer your trust to
Him, you repent and turn to Him, you cling to Him, and you rely upon
Him for every minute of every day. His riches are yours when you

believe, and you need to call on Him to begin writing checks from his fathomless wealth.

I'm not talking about money here, I'm talking about the wealth of true spirituality—what money can't buy and death can't take away. Jesus said that he and the Father are one and you are safe within His hands. So no one can snatch you from Jesus's hands once you believe in Him, and no one can snatch you from the Father's hands either.

I'm also talking about the blessing of health, family, and friends along with having joy and peace. You don't have to look far to see how incredibly blessed you are.

I recommend that you find a church that believes and teaches the Bible and meet up with a group of Christian friends on a regular basis to sharpen your faith. Prayer, reading your Bible, and worshipping God are all ways to help that flow of living water stream from your innermost being.

I now pray for you, "Spring up oh well! Spring up and flow rivers of living water! Be born again today by believing in Jesus. As you have received Him, so walk in Him. I want you to store up riches in heaven so that you are wealthy in things that money cannot buy and death cannot take away. Discover true wealth today and experience Christ in you, your hope of glory."

CHAPTER 20

THE #1 MOST-IMPORTANT COMPONENT OF A WEALTH PLAN

WE GUIDE AND HELP YOU DECIDE

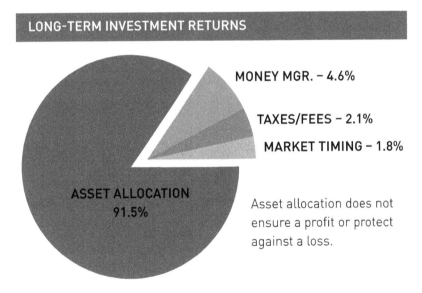

Brinson, Singer, Beebower, "Determinants of Portfolio Performance II: An Update"
Financial Analysts Journal, 5-6/1991

In 1986, asset allocation researcher Gilbert Beebower and others produced a landmark paper titled "Determinants of Portfolio Performance," in which the authors concluded that the primary determinant of a portfolio's performance was asset allocation.

While the findings have been a much-debated topic ever since, Peter Lynch, the well-regarded former manager of Fidelity Magellan, wrote in his book *Beating the Street* that the most important decision is the original stock-versus-bond decision. In other words, your risk tolerance decision: How much do you have in stocks versus bonds?

We see this as the most important component of building a wealth plan—the understanding of your risk tolerance—and we begin every client relationship with a series of conversations to gain insight into the factors that drive your decisions.

Foremost of these is what we call the "expectations conversation." In this conversation, we want to learn about what you expect from working with an advisor like me.

When it comes to knowing how to serve you, the most important thing for us is to understand your expectations and how to meet those. Learning your initial stock-versus-bond decision is of primary importance in understanding your needs—that's your risk tolerance in building the investment portfolio.

What it boils down to is expectations. It's just like any relationship. For example, if you're married and your spouse expects you home at 6:00 p.m. and you get there at 7:00 p.m., your spouse may get upset because you violated his or her expectations.

The same is true of an advisor: it's important for you to understand your expectations so that you can be served well. Your advisor needs to understand your risk tolerance and then build your estate plan, your retirement plan, or your asset protection plan upon what's important to you, your goals, and your objectives.

Together, you'll formulate a picture of what your relationship should look like—what you should expect from your advisor and what your advisor should expect of you—and then you can put together guidelines that you both agree to abide by.

This starts with the understanding that the most important aspect of the relationship is to know and appreciate each other's expectations. Then you can develop a really great relationship, with your retirement wealth advisor serving you the way you want to be served.

In order to design a comprehensive plan, your advisor also needs to understand your values. Then he or she can build a family wealth plan that is fulfilling for you because it is about more than just money—it is about family, mission, ministry, or whatever else is most important to you.

Once your advisor understands your risk tolerance and your values, he or she can build a customized retirement road map and wealth plan using the Eight Investment Strategies for Life.

THE VALUES ELICITATION CONVERSATION

Life coach Doug Carter has compiled a list of questions that we like to use as part of what is termed a "values elicitation conversation."

You'll need a blank sheet of paper and a writing instrument.

On the paper, draw a large letter *T*, and above the top line of the *T* (the crossbar) write the question "What's important about life to you?"

In the space below the crossbar, on the left side of the stem of the *T*, list 6 to 12 intangible values that are important to you, such as love, family, security, spirituality, and philanthropy. Make sure they are values that are important to you, not to someone else, because we want to be sure the strategies we put together are right for you.

Next, prioritize the values as you move them to a list on the right side of the *T* stem. For example, if family is the most important item in the list on the left, then make it item A in the list on the right side of the stem. If spirituality is second, list it as item B.

Think of the exercise as similar to baking a cake. You need the basic ingredients—flour, baking soda, and so on—in other words, the values that you feel are most important, most essential to a fulfilling life. Then decide which values are essentially the "icing on the cake" or give the cake its flavor, such as apple spice or cinnamon. Which of the values that you listed enhance your quality of life?

An important note in doing this exercise is to recognize that values can shift. A significant event like death, finding a life partner, or a threat from natural or manmade sources can cause people to reevaluate their values.

Values are feelings. The words in the list are not the values; they're triggers to your emotional understanding of those values.

THE INTERVIEW

We follow Doug Carter's values elicitation conversation with what we call the "innerview." Through a set of 25 questions about a person's working life, educational background, recreational interests, family situation, upbringing, influences, and treasured memories, we get to know more about each client and some of the factors that may have shaped the person's values.

The goal in building an investment plan is to know what's important in life to each client and to gain an understanding of what role money plays in his or her values. This helps us determine expectations and risk tolerance.

In order to build an investment plan for you, we need to know what you're about, what you think of money, and what you value in life.

Together, imagining financial wealth will no longer be a dream, it will be a reality to help you feel secure for life.

NOTE: to reach Doug Carter, you can email or call him at: clientsforever@sbcglobal.net, 1-530-926-3782

CHAPTER 20 TAKEAWAYS:

THE 25 INNERVIEW QUESTIONS

1. What exactly do you do?

2. How long have you been doing this?

3. How did you get started?

4. What do you like best about your work?

5. What would you change about it if you could?

6. What kind of educational background do you have?

7. What do you do besides work? Sports, clubs, causes?

8. What's your family situation? Relationship? Children? Close or distant?

9. Where are you from originally?

10. What was your family situation like when you were growing up? Siblings, family structure, where were they in the birth order?

11. What was that like?

12. What was it like around the dinner table when you were growing up?

13. Were you actively involved in school? (sports, politics, clubs, etc.)

14. What's one memory that really stands out?

15. Most people have had at least one person who really seemed to make a difference in their lives. Who was that person for you?

16. What did you learn from them?

17. What impact has this had on your life? (15-17 do loop)

18. If you look at your life like a "radar scope," there will no doubt be some "ups" and some "downs." What's one of the ups for you?

19. What does that tell you about yourself?

20. What was one of the downs?

21. What got you through that?

22. If you could "roll the clock back" to before this incident took place, what would you have done differently?

23. Let's say you had a young person here (providing of course they would listen to you). And they asked you what lessons life has taught you...what would you tell them?

24. What taught you that?

25. What does the future hold for you now?

APPENDIX I

THE HANDOUTS TYPICALLY GIVEN OUT AT WORKSHOPS.

THE WELSHIRE CAPITAL^{SM} CONFIDENTIAL PERSONAL & FINANCIAL PROFILE

Confidential Personal & Financial Profile

CONFIDENTIAL PERSONAL PROFILE

This comprehensive, personal financial planning summary is designed to help you take inventory and assign realistic values to your personal assets and liabilities. It's the essential first step in organizing a sensible financial plan for your future.

Checklist of documents to bring to initial consultation:

☐ Confidential Profile   ☐ All annuity, life & long-term care policies
☐ Last year's tax return   ☐ All IRA & retirement statements
☐ All brokerage firm statements   ☐ Copies of wills & trusts

Family Information

Your Name _____ Age _____ Birthdate _____ Social Security # _____

Spouse's Name _____ Age _____ Birthdate _____ Social Security # _____

Residence Address _____ City _____ State _____ Zip _____

Mailing Address _____ City _____ State _____ Zip _____

Home Phone _____ Fax# _____ E-mail _____

Children's Names	Age	State of Residence	# of Grandchildren
1.			
2.			
3.			
4.			
5.			

Occupation

Your Job Title _____ Employer (last, if retired) _____

# of years _____ Work Phone _____ Retirement Date _____

Spouse's Job Title _____ Employer (last, if retired) _____

# of years _____ Work Phone _____ Retirement Date _____

Advisors

Financial Advisor's Name _____ Firm Name _____ City _____ State _____
Do you have a preference or a commitment to this advisor? ☐ Yes ☐ No

Attorney's Name _____ Firm Name _____ City _____ State _____
Do you have a preference or a commitment to this advisor? ☐ Yes ☐ No

Accountant's Name _____ Firm Name _____ City _____ State _____
Do you have a preference or a commitment to this advisor? ☐ Yes ☐ No

Insurance Agent's Name _____ Firm Name _____ City _____ State _____
Do you have a preference or a commitment to this advisor? ☐ Yes ☐ No

Stock Broker's Name _____ Firm Name _____ City _____ State _____
Do you have a preference or a commitment to this advisor? ☐ Yes ☐ No

Please complete this questionnaire to the best of your ability. It's difficult to know if you're going the right direction—if you don't know where you'd like to go.

CONFIDENTIAL PERSONAL GOALS PROFILE

---

1. Five years from today, how do you expect your household annual income to change?

   ☐ To grow substantially   ☐ To decrease substantially
   ☐ To grow moderately   ☐ To decrease moderately
   ☐ To stay about the same

2. With income generated from your portfolio for the next _____ years, you plan to:

   ☐ Use it for living expenses   ☐ Reinvest all income
   ☐ Use some and reinvest some

3. Five years from today, how do you expect your portfolio value to change?

   ☐ Portfolio is not my primary concern. I am more concerned with current income
   ☐ The same as or slightly more than today
   ☐ Greater than today
   ☐ Substantially greater than today

4. In the 20th Century, inflation existed in 97 years of 100. What is your realistic rate of return goal for your overall portfolio as compared to inflation?

   ☐ Beat inflation by 2% per year   ☐ Beat inflation by 6% per year
   ☐ Beat inflation by 4% per year   ☐ Beat inflation by ___ per year

5. Items with which you would like assistance. (Check all that apply)

   ☐ Increase my standard of living   ☐ Pay for college education for children
   ☐ Financial security at retirement   ☐ Provide for my family in the event of my death
   ☐ Increase my net worth by ___%   ☐ Minimize the cost of probate & estate taxes
   ☐ Reduce my tax burden   ☐ Control the distribution of my assets to my heirs
   ☐ Simplify my financial affairs   ☐ Plan for home health care/nursing home care

6. How much income do you want from your portfolio during your retirement years? $_____/year.

7. Other Goals: _____

   _____

8. If you could change two things about your current financial situation, what would you change?

   1. _____   2. _____

INCOME STATEMENT

For the year beginning January 1, _____ and ending December 31, _____.

Wages of Salary .... Combined _____ Husband _____ Wife _____

Social Security Income .... Combined _____ Husband _____ Wife _____

Pensions .... Combined _____ Husband _____ Wife _____

Dividend and Interest .... Combined _____ Husband _____ Wife _____

Capital Gains & Losses .... Combined _____ Husband _____ Wife _____
(e.g., sale of stock)

Rents, Annuities, etc. .... Combined _____ Husband _____ Wife _____

Other .... _____

Total Annual Income .... _____

BALANCE SHEET

Assets

Monetary Assets

1. Cash
   On Hand .... _____
   Checking Account .... _____
   Savings Account .... _____
   Money Market .... _____
   Certificates of Deposit .... _____

   TOTAL CASH: .... _____

2. Investments
   Savings Bonds .... _____
   Stocks and Bonds .... _____
   Mutual Funds .... _____
   Cash Value of Life Insurance .... _____
   Cash Value of Annuities .... _____
   IRA's .... _____
   401(k) Retirement Accounts .... _____
   Money loaned to others (repayment expected) .... _____
   Other .... _____

   TOTAL INVESTMENTS: .... _____

3. TOTAL MONETARY ASSETS: (Sum of 1 and 2) .... _____

Fixed Assets

4. Home and Property .... _____
5. Other Real Estate Investments .... _____
6. Automobiles .... _____
7. Ownership Interest in Small Business .... _____
8. Personal Property .... _____
9. Total Fixed Assets .... _____
10. Total Assets: (Sum of 3 and 9) .... _____

Liabilities

11. Unpaid Bills
    Taxes .... _____
    Insurance Premiums .... _____
    Rent .... _____
    Utilities .... _____
    Charge Accounts .... _____
    Other .... _____

    TOTAL UNPAID BILLS .... _____

12. Installment Loans (balance due)

    Mortgage Loans .... _____
    Automobile 1 .... _____
    Automobile 2 .... _____
    Bank Loan .... _____
    Credit Cards .... _____
    Educational .... _____
    Other .... _____

    TOTAL LOANS .... _____

13. TOTAL LIABILITIES: (Sum of 11 and 12) .... _____

NET WORTH OF FAMILY (Subtract 13 from 10):

3 of 4

INVESTMENT GOALS

	Low Priority						High Priority			
1. Long term growth: My return should exceed inflation rate.	1	2	3	4	5	6	7	8	9	10
2. Safety: I want my principal to be safe.	1	2	3	4	5	6	7	8	9	10
3. Current Income: I want to spend all my portfolio gains.	1	2	3	4	5	6	7	8	9	10
4. Income Taxes: I want my income taxes reduced.	1	2	3	4	5	6	7	8	9	10
5. Estate Taxes: I want my estate taxes minimized.	1	2	3	4	5	6	7	8	9	10
6. Liquidity: My principal should be immediately accessible.	1	2	3	4	5	6	7	8	9	10
7. Diversification: I want a sound asset allocation strategy.	1	2	3	4	5	6	7	8	9	10
8. Financial Advisor: I want professional management.	1	2	3	4	5	6	7	8	9	10

	Low Risk						High Risk			
9. Rate your risk tolerance level.	1	2	3	4	5	6	7	8	9	10

WHAT IS IMPORTANT ABOUT MONEY TO YOU?

NOTES:

APPENDIX II

Dalbar's Quantitative Analysis of Investor Behavior (QAIB)

Allianz Life Insurance Company of North America, *Reclaiming the Future Study*, accessed December 28, 2014, https://www.allianzlife.com/retirement-and-planning-tools/reclaiming-the-future/white-paper-findings.

Kelly, Patrick. *Stress-Free Retirement*. Rubicon, 2013.

Pension Benefit Guaranty Corporation (PBGC) Annual Report Fiscal Year 2014, (Washington, D.C.: PBGC, 2014).

Quante, Don. *Don't Go Broke in a Nursing Home*. St. Charles: AFFC Publications. 2013.

Welch, Brent. "Two More Bubbles," *Financial Health*. July 2014.

Brent Welch has been helping his clients retire with confidence for more than three decades. He is the founder and managing member of Welshire Capital^{SM}, LLC, a firm focusing on private wealth management, retirement, and estate planning for more than 500 families in more than a dozen states.

He is past president of the International Forum, past board member for the Association for Advanced Life Underwriting (AALU) of Washington, D.C., a Qualified and Life Member of the Million Dollar Round Table, and a Top of the Table member for more than a dozen years. At the time of this writing, Welch serves on the Million Dollar Round Table's finance, communications, and sales and marketing committees. He is also a board member of the Christian Study Group and a 12-year member of the Cayman Study Group. Welch used to serve as an elder in his church and was a lead worshipper at his church for a couple decades.

Welch is the author of a previous book on financial planning: *Financial Planning, Practice Standards and Ethics*, published by the Singapore College of Insurance in 2004.

Majoring in finance at the University of Wisconsin-La Crosse, Welch received a certificate in Bible studies from Capernwray Bible School in Carnforth, LANCS, England. He is a Certified Financial Planner®, Chartered Retirement Plan Specialist®, Chartered Financial Consultant, Chartered Life Underwriter, and an Accredited Investment Fiduciary®. He has been called upon to speak at various financial conventions including the Singapore College of Insurance Third Annual Financial Planning Conference, the AIA Sales Congress in Singapore, the AIG conference in Kuala Lumpur, Malaysia, the Million Dollar Round Table, and the National Association of Insurance and Financial Advisors.

Welch credits his father, in part, for the way he works with clients. "I learned from my dad back in 1984 that I needed to provide options for clients. He was my first client, and I did an insurance review with recommendations for him. But he wouldn't take my recommendations. He wanted to see some options," Welch says. Creating a menu of options or recommendations for clients to choose from has become Welshire's^{SM} philosophy of "We Guide and Help You Decide."

Welch became a wealth manager because he just wanted to do something that helps people. He continues to help people work toward retiring with confidence and peace through his business, books, public classes and seminars, speaking engagements, and radio show, "Retirement Readiness Radio" RetirementReadiness-Radio.com. His blog is under construction at FamilyWealth.com.

Welshire^{SM} hosts dozens of classes in LaCrosse and Madison to help educate people between the ages of 54 to 70 to help make smarter choices with their money. His students are in charge of their retirement, and they deserve to know answers to questions such as "Do I have enough?," "Will I run out?," "Am I on track?" Welch is a Dave Ramsey ELP Endorsed Local Provider in the Eau Claire, Wisconsin, area. Visit Welshire.com for more information about dates, times, and locations.

Welch has been married since 1986 and has three children. He is passionate about his faith, family, friends, having fun, and being philanthropic. He enjoys prayer, worship, drumming, music, art, golfing, fishing, hunting, boating, and spending time with family and friends at his cabin up north.

WHY? WHY DOES WELSHIRE^{SM} EXIST?

MISSION & PASSION

Welshire^{SM} Capital's mission is to help you retire with confidence and peace.

WHAT? WHAT IS WELSHIRE DOING THAT CAN MAKE A DIFFERENCE THAT YOU CAN EXPERIENCE IN YOUR LIFE?

VALUE PROPOSITION

- Welshire^{SM} Retirement Planning—*helping you retire with confidence and peace*

- Welshire^{SM} Asset Protection—*helping you keep together what you've worked so hard to put together*

- Welshire's^{SM} 8 Investment Strategies—*we guide and help you decide*

- Welshire^{SM} Services—*serving you the way we want to be served*

HOW? HOW DOES WELSHIRE^{SM} ADD VALUE TO YOUR LIFE?

WELSHIRE'S^{SM} CLIENT BILL OF RIGHTS

- Clients have the right to be served the way they want to be served.

- Clients have the right to transparent, proactive service.

- Clients have the right to abundant communication and education.

- Clients have the right to get a person on the phone when they call and not a recording.

- Clients deserve to have their phone calls and emails returned promptly, thoroughly, and accurately.

- Clients are in charge of their retirement and deserve help to make smarter choices with their money.

- Clients should have their needs and wishes met with genuine care.

- Clients have the right to become raving fans of Welshire[SM] and introduce their family and friends.

WELSHIRE'S[SM] ETHICS INITIATIVE

- Being accountable through various organizations such as:

  - Character First Curriculum for the Welshire[SM] Team
  - Marketplace Leaders devotionals
  - Better Business Bureau
  - Chamber of commerce
  - Ethics.net
  - MDRT.org
  - NAIFA.org
  - CFP board of standards
  - ChFC, CLU, CRPS Boards through the American College
  - AIF board through fi360.com
  - FINRA.gov
  - SEC.gov

WELSHIRE'S[SM] EDUCATIONAL AND COMMUNICATION INITIATIVE

- Daily AssetLock technology monitoring available

- Welshire[SM] Weekly Commentary

- Retirement Readiness Radio

- Monthly "Life Notes" newsletter

- Periodic classes, seminars, workshops, or client events

- Monthly e-statements

- Brent's prerecorded market message

- Quarterly investment summaries available

- Periodic annual or semi-annual meetings or when needed

- Periodic phone calls

- The whole team is available for YOU every working day

- Four Meeting Process: Discovery, Planning, Implementation, and Review

NOTE: WELSHIRE^{SM} RESERVES THE RIGHT TO DO RANDOM ACTS OF KINDNESS AND CHANGE OR IMPROVE YOUR SERVICE AT ANY TIME UNANNOUNCED.

ABOUT
RETIREMENT READINESS RADIO

Brent Welch shares his knowledge and insights about the road to financial security on the Retirement Readiness Radio program. Please review archived audio recordings and other information at:

www.RetirementReadinessRadio.com

401(K) PLAN

A qualified retirement plan available to eligible employees of companies. 401(k) plans allow eligible employees to defer taxation on a specific percentage of their income that is to be put toward retirement savings; taxes on this deferred income and on any earnings the account generates are deferred until the funds are withdrawn—normally in retirement. Employers may match part or all of an employee's contributions. Employees may be responsible for investment selections and enjoy the direct tax savings. ROTH 401(k) plans are potentially tax-free accounts that are funded with after-tax contributions. If you hold a ROTH 401(k) for five years and to age 59 ½, the investment gains may be totally tax free.

403(B) PLAN

A 403(b) plan is similar to a 401(k). A 403(b) is a qualified retirement plan available to employees of nonprofit and government organizations.

AFTER-TAX RETURN

The return on an investment after subtracting any taxes due.

AGGRESSIVE GROWTH FUND

A mutual fund offered by an investment company that specifically pursues substantial capital gains. Mutual fund balances are subject to fluctuation in value and market risk. Shares, when redeemed, may be worth more or less than their original cost. Mutual funds are sold only by prospectus. Individuals are encouraged to consider the charges, risks, expenses, and investment objectives carefully before investing. A prospectus containing this and other information about the investment company can be obtained from your financial professional. Read it carefully before you invest or send money.

ANNUITY

A contract with an insurance company that guarantees current or future payments in exchange for a premium or series of premiums. The interest earned on an annuity contract is not taxable until the funds are paid out or withdrawn. Withdrawals and income payments are taxed as ordinary income. If a withdrawal is made prior to age 59½, penalties may apply. The guarantees of an annuity contract depend on the issuing company's claims-paying ability. Annuities have fees and charges associated with the contract, and a surrender charge also may apply if the contract owner elects to give up the annuity before certain time-period conditions are satisfied.

ASSET ALLOCATION

A method of allocating funds to pursue the highest potential return at a specific level of risk. Asset allocation normally uses sophisticated mathematical analysis of the historical performance of asset classes to attempt to project future risk and return. Asset allocation is an approach to help manage investment risk. It does not guarantee against investment loss.

BALANCED MUTUAL FUND

A mutual fund offered by an investment company which attempts to hold a balance of stocks and bonds. Mutual funds are subject to fluctuation in value and market risk. Shares, when redeemed, may be worth more or less than their original cost. Mutual funds are sold only by prospectus. Individuals are encouraged to consider the charges, risks, expenses, and investment objectives carefully before investing. A prospectus containing this and other information about the investment company can be obtained from your financial professional. Read it carefully before you invest or send money.

BEAR MARKET

A market experiencing an extended period of declining prices. A bear market is the opposite of a bull market.

BENEFICIARY

The person or entity who will receive benefits from a life insurance policy, qualified retirement plan, annuity, trust, or will upon the death of an individual.

BLUE CHIP STOCK

The stock of an established company that has a history of generating a profit and possibly a consistent dividend.

BOND

A debt instrument under which the issuer promises to pay a specified amount of interest and to repay the principal at maturity. The market value of a bond will fluctuate with changes in interest rates. As rates rise, the value of existing bonds typically falls. If an investor sells a bond before maturity, it may be worth more or less than the initial purchase price. By holding a bond to maturity, an investor will receive the interest payments due plus his or her original principal, barring default by the issuer. Investments seeking to achieve higher yields also involve a higher degree of risk.

BULL MARKET

A market experiencing an extended period of rising prices. A bull market is the opposite of a bear market.

CAPITAL GAIN OR LOSS

The difference between the price at which an asset was purchased and the price for which it was sold. When the sale price is higher than the purchase price, the difference is a capital gain; when the sale price is lower than the purchase price, the difference is a capital loss.

CERTIFICATE OF DEPOSIT (CD)

A deposit with a bank, thrift institution, or credit union that promises a fixed interest rate on funds deposited for a specified period of time. Bank savings accounts and CDs are FDIC insured up to $250,000 per depositor per institution and generally provide a fixed rate of return, whereas the value of money market mutual funds can fluctuate.

DEBT-TO-EQUITY RATIO

The ratio of a company's total debt to its total shareholder equity. Some use the debt-to-equity ratio to attempt to ascertain a company's capability to repay its creditors.

DEFERRED ANNUITY

A contract with an insurance company that guarantees a future payment or series of payments in exchange for current premiums. The interest earned on an annuity contract is not taxable until the funds are paid out or withdrawn. The guarantees of an annuity contract depend on the issuing company's claims-paying ability. Annuities have fees and charges associated with the contract, and a surrender charge also may apply if the contract owner elects to give up the annuity before certain time-period conditions are satisfied.

DIVERSIFICATION

An investment strategy under which capital is divided among several assets or asset classes. Diversification operates under the assumption that different assets and/or asset classes are unlikely to move in the same direction, allowing gains in one investment to offset losses in another. Diversification is an approach to help manage investment risk. It does not eliminate the risk of loss if security prices decline.

DIVIDEND

Taxable payments made by a company to its shareholders. Some dividends are paid quarterly and others are paid monthly. Companies can adjust common share dividends at any time, pending approval by the company's board of directors.

DOW JONES INDUSTRIAL AVERAGE (DJIA)

An average calculated by summing the prices of 30 actively leading stocks on the New York Stock Exchange (NYSE) and dividing the sum by a divisor which has been adjusted to account for cases of stock splits, spinoffs, or similar structural changes. Individuals cannot invest directly in an index.

ESTATE TAX

Federal and/or state taxes that may be levied on the assets of a deceased person upon his or her death. These taxes are paid by the deceased person's estate rather than his or her heirs.

EXCHANGE-TRADED FUNDS (ETFS)

A share of an investment company that owns a block of shares selected to pursue a specific investment objective. ETFs trade like stocks and are listed on stock exchanges and sold by broker-dealers. Exchange-traded funds are sold only by prospectus. Consider the charges, risks, expenses, and investment objectives carefully before investing. A prospectus containing this and other information about the investment company can be obtained from your financial professional. Read it carefully before you invest or send money.

FEDERAL RESERVE SYSTEM (THE FED)

The United States' central bank. The Federal Reserve System consists of a series of 12 independent banks that operate under the supervision of a seven-member, federally appointed board of governors. The Fed strives to maintain maximum employment, stable price levels, and moderate long-term interest rates. It establishes and enforces the regulations that banks, savings and loans, and credit unions must follow. It also acts as a clearing house for certain financial transactions and provides banking services to the federal government.

FIXED ANNUITY

A contract with an insurance company that guarantees investment growth at a fixed interest rate as well as current or future payments in exchange for a premium or series of premiums. The interest earned on an annuity contract is not taxable until the funds are paid out or withdrawn. The guarantees of an annuity contract depend on the issuing company's claims-paying ability. Annuities have fees and charges associated with the contract, and a surrender charge also may apply if the contract owner elects to give up the annuity before certain time-period conditions are satisfied.

FIXED INDEX ANNUITY

A fixed index annuity offers returns based on the changes in a securities index, such as the S&P 500 Composite Stock Price Index. Indexed annuity contracts also offer a specified minimum that the contract value will not fall below, regardless of index performance. After a period of time, the insurance company will make payments to you under the terms of your contract. A fixed index annuity is not a stock market investment and does not directly participate in any stock or equity investment. It may be appropriate for individuals who want guaranteed interest rates and the potential for lifetime income. Lifetime income may be provided through the purchase of an optional rider for an additional cost or through annuitization at no additional cost.

When discussing annuities, it's important to remember that all guarantees and protections are subject to the claims-paying ability of the issuing company.

INDEX

An average of the prices of a hypothetical basket of securities representing a particular market or portion of a market. Among the best-known indexes are the Dow Jones Industrials Index (the Dow), the Standard & Poor's 500 Index (S&P 500), and the Russell 2000 Index. Index performance is not indicative of the past performance of a particular investment. Past performance does not guarantee future results. Individuals cannot invest directly in an index.

INDIVIDUAL RETIREMENT ACCOUNT (IRA)

A qualified retirement account for individuals. Contributions to a traditional IRA may be fully or partially deductible, depending on your individual circumstance. Distributions from traditional IRA and most other employer-sponsored retirement plans are taxed as ordinary income and, if taken before age 59½, may be subject to a 10 percent federal income tax penalty. Generally, once you reach age 70½, you must begin taking required minimum distributions.

INFLATION

An upward movement in the average level of prices. Each month, the Bureau of Labor Statistics reports on the average level of prices when it releases the Consumer Price Index (CPI).

INTEREST RATE

The cost to borrow money expressed as a percentage of the loan amount over one year.

IRREVOCABLE TRUST

A trust that cannot be altered, stopped, or canceled after its creation without the permission of the beneficiary or trustee. Using a trust involves a complex set of tax rules and regulations. Before moving forward with a trust, consider working with a professional who is familiar with the rules and regulations.

LIFE INSURANCE

A contract under which an insurance company promises, in exchange for premiums, to pay a set benefit when the policyholder dies. Several factors will affect the cost and availability of life insurance, including age, health, and the type and amount of insurance purchased. Life insurance policies have expenses, including mortality and other charges. If a policy is surrendered prematurely, the policyholder also may pay surrender charges and have income tax implications. You should consider determining whether you are insurable before implementing a strategy involving life insurance. Any guarantees associated with a policy are dependent on the ability of the issuing insurance company to continue making claim payments.

LIQUIDITY

The ease and speed with which an asset or security can be bought or sold.

LIVING TRUST

A trust created by a living person that allows that person to control the assets he or she contributes to the trust during his or her lifetime and to direct their disposition upon his or her death.

LONG-TERM CARE INSURANCE

Insurance that covers the cost of medical and nonmedical services needed by those who have a chronic illness or disability—most commonly associated with aging. Long-term care insurance can cover the cost of nursing home care, in-home assistance, assisted living, and adult day care.

MANAGEMENT FEE

The cost of having assets professionally managed. This fee is normally a fixed percentage of the fund's asset value; terms of the fee are disclosed in the prospectus. These fees may also be found in a Registered Investment Advisor's ADV-2.

MARITAL DEDUCTION

A provision of the tax code that allows an individual to transfer an unlimited amount of assets to his or her spouse at any time—including upon the individual's death—without triggering a tax liability.

MARKET RISK

The risk that an entire market will decline, reducing the value of the investments in it without regard to other factors. This is also known as "systemic risk."

MATURITY

The date on which a debt security comes due for payment and on which an investor's principal is due to be repaid.

MONEY MARKET FUND

A mutual fund that invests in assets that are easily converted into cash and which have a low risk of price fluctuation. This may include money market holdings, Treasury bills, and commercial paper. Money held in money market funds is not insured or guaranteed by the Federal Deposit Insurance Corporation or any other government agency. Money market funds seek to preserve the value of your investment at $1.00 a share. However, it is possible to lose money by investing in a money market fund.

MUTUAL FUND

A pooled investment account offered by an investment company. Mutual funds pool the monies of many investors and then invest the money to pursue the fund's stated objectives. The resulting portfolio of investments is managed by the investment company. Mutual fund balances are subject to fluctuation in value and market risk. Shares, when redeemed, may be worth more or less that their original cost. Mutual funds are sold only by prospectus. Individuals are encouraged to consider the charges, risks, expenses, and investment objectives carefully before investing. A prospectus containing this and other information about the investment company can be obtained from your financial professional. Read it carefully before you invest or send money.

NATIONAL ASSOCIATION OF SECURITIES DEALERS AUTOMATED QUOTATIONS (NASDAQ)

An American stock exchange originally founded by the National Association of Securities Dealers. When the NASDAQ stock exchange began trading on February 8, 1971, it was the world's first electronic stock market.

NET ASSET VALUE

The net market value of a mutual fund's current holdings divided by the number of outstanding shares. The product of this division estimates the per-share value of the fund's assets.

NET INCOME

A company's total revenues minus its costs, expenses, and taxes. Net income is the bottom line of a company's income statement (which may also be called the profit and loss statement).

NEW YORK STOCK EXCHANGE (NYSE)

A stock exchange located on Wall Street in New York City, NY. Many regard the NYSE as the largest exchange in the United States and possibly the world.

POLICY RIDER

A provision to a life insurance policy that is purchased separately from the basic policy and that provides additional benefits at additional cost.

PREFERRED STOCK

Securities that represent ownership in a corporation and have a higher claim on a company's assets and earnings than common stock. Dividends on preferred stock are generally paid out before dividends to common stockholders.

PRINCIPAL

The original amount invested in a security, excluding earnings; the face value of a bond; or the remaining amount owed on a loan, separate from interest.

PROSPECTUS

A legal document that provides the information an investor needs to make an informed decision about an investment offered for sale to the public. Prospectuses are required by and filed with the Securities and Exchange Commission.

RATE OF RETURN

A measure of the performance of an investment. Rate of return is calculated by dividing any gain or loss by an investment's initial cost. Rates of return usually account for any income received from the investment in addition to any realized capital gains.

REAL ESTATE INVESTMENT TRUST (REIT)

A pooled investment that invests primarily in real estate. REITs trade like stocks on the major exchanges. Keep in mind that the return and principal value of REIT prices will fluctuate as market conditions change. And shares, when sold, may be worth more or less than their original cost.

REQUIRED MINIMUM DISTRIBUTION (RMD)

The amount which must be withdrawn annually from a qualified retirement plan beginning April 1 of the year following the year in which the account holder reaches age 70½.

REVOCABLE TRUST

A trust that can be altered or canceled by its grantor. During the life of the trust, any income earned is distributed to the grantor; upon the grantor's death, the contents of the trust are transferred to its beneficiaries according to the terms of the trust.

RISK TOLERANCE

A measurement of an investor's willingness or ability to handle investment losses.

ROTH IRA

A qualified retirement plan in which earnings grow tax deferred and distributions are tax free. Contributions to a Roth IRA are generally not deductible for tax purposes, and there are income and contribution limits. Roth IRA contributions cannot be made by taxpayers with high incomes. To qualify for the tax-free and penalty-free withdrawal of earnings, Roth IRA distributions must meet a five-year holding requirement and occur after age 59½. Tax-free and penalty-free withdrawal also can be taken under certain other circumstances, such as after the owner's death. The original Roth IRA owner is not required to take minimum annual withdrawals.

ROTH IRA CONVERSION

The process of transferring assets from a traditional, SEP, or SIMPLE IRA to a Roth IRA. Roth IRA conversions are subject to specific requirements and may be taxable.

SECURITIES AND EXCHANGE COMMISSION (SEC)

A federal agency with a mandate to protect investors; to maintain fair, orderly, and efficient markets; and to facilitate capital formation. The SEC acts as one of the primary regulatory agencies for the investment industry.

SELF-DIRECTED IRA

An individual retirement arrangement in which the account holder can direct the investment of funds, subject to certain conditions and limits.

SHARE

A unit of ownership in a corporation or financial asset.

STANDARD & POOR'S 500 INDEX (S&P 500)

An average calculated by summing the prices of 500 leading companies in leading industries of the US economy and dividing the sum by a divisor which is regularly adjusted to account for stock splits, spinoffs, or similar structural changes. Index performance is not indicative of the past performance of a particular investment. Past performance does not guarantee future results. Individuals cannot invest directly in an index.

STOCK

An equity investment in a company. Stockholders own a share of the company and are entitled to any dividends and financial participation in company growth. They also have the right to vote on the company's board of directors. Keep in mind that the return and principal value of stock prices will fluctuate as market conditions change. And shares, when sold, may be worth more or less than their original cost.

STOCK CERTIFICATE

A legal document that certifies ownership of a specific number of shares of stock in a corporation. In many transactions, the stockholder is registered electronically, and no certificate is issued.

TAX DEFERRED

A condition of certain plans and accounts under which the funds in the plan or account, along with any accrued interest, dividends, or other capital gains, are not subject to taxes until the funds are withdrawn.

TECHNICAL ANALYSIS

A method of evaluating securities by examining recent price movements and trends in an attempt to identify patterns that can suggest future activity. Generally, technical analysis is the opposite of fundamental analysis.

TIME HORIZON

The amount of time an investor plans to hold an investment or portfolio of investments.

TREASURIES

Debt securities issued by the US government. Treasury bills normally have maturities of less than one year, Treasury notes have maturities between 1 and 10 years, and Treasury bonds have maturities between 10 and 30 years. US Treasury securities are guaranteed by the federal government as to the timely payment of principal and interest. However, if you sell a Treasury security prior to maturity, it could be worth more or less than the original price paid.

TRUST

A trust is a legal arrangement that creates a separate entity which can own property and is managed for the benefit of a beneficiary. A living trust is created while its grantor is still alive. A testamentary trust is created upon the grantor's death—usually by another trust or by a will. Using a trust involves a complex set of tax rules and regulations. Before moving forward with a trust, consider working with a professional who is familiar with the rules and regulations.

UNLIMITED MARITAL DEDUCTION

A provision of the tax code that allows an individual to transfer an unlimited amount of assets to his or her spouse at any time—including upon the individual's death—without triggering a tax liability.

VARIABLE INTEREST RATE

An interest rate that moves up and down with a specific measure or index, such as current money market rates or a lender's cost of funds.

'UITY

...tion of a variable annuity is as follows, "A variable ⌐ a contract between you and an insurance company, under .ch you make a lump-sum payment or a series of payments. In return, the insurer agrees to make periodic payments to you beginning immediately or at some future day. You can choose to invest your purchase payments in a range of investment options, which are typically mutual funds. The value of your account in a vaiable annuity will vary; depending on the performance of the investment options you have chosen."

VOLATILITY

A measure of the range of potential fluctuations in a security's value. A higher volatility means the security's value can potentially fluctuate over a larger range of potential outcomes—up and down.

YIELD

A measure of the performance of an investment. Yield is calculated by dividing the income received from an investment by the investment's initial cost. Yield differs from rate of return in that it accounts only for income; rate of return also includes appreciation or depreciation in the value of the investment.

9 781599 325774

TREASURIES

Debt securities issued by the US government. Treasury bills normally have maturities of less than one year, Treasury notes have maturities between 1 and 10 years, and Treasury bonds have maturities between 10 and 30 years. US Treasury securities are guaranteed by the federal government as to the timely payment of principal and interest. However, if you sell a Treasury security prior to maturity, it could be worth more or less than the original price paid.

TRUST

A trust is a legal arrangement that creates a separate entity which can own property and is managed for the benefit of a beneficiary. A living trust is created while its grantor is still alive. A testamentary trust is created upon the grantor's death—usually by another trust or by a will. Using a trust involves a complex set of tax rules and regulations. Before moving forward with a trust, consider working with a professional who is familiar with the rules and regulations.

UNLIMITED MARITAL DEDUCTION

A provision of the tax code that allows an individual to transfer an unlimited amount of assets to his or her spouse at any time—including upon the individual's death—without triggering a tax liability.

VARIABLE INTEREST RATE

An interest rate that moves up and down with a specific measure or index, such as current money market rates or a lender's cost of funds.

VARIABLE ANNUITY

The SEC definition of a variable annuity is as follows, "A variable annuity is a contract between you and an insurance company, under which you make a lump-sum payment or a series of payments. In return, the insurer agrees to make periodic payments to you beginning immediately or at some future day. You can choose to invest your purchase payments in a range of investment options, which are typically mutual funds. The value of your account in a vaiable annuity will vary; depending on the performance of the investment options you have chosen."

VOLATILITY

A measure of the range of potential fluctuations in a security's value. A higher volatility means the security's value can potentially fluctuate over a larger range of potential outcomes—up and down.

YIELD

A measure of the performance of an investment. Yield is calculated by dividing the income received from an investment by the investment's initial cost. Yield differs from rate of return in that it accounts only for income; rate of return also includes appreciation or depreciation in the value of the investment.